Basic Intensive Psychotherapy

Also by William H. Reid

*The Psychopath: A Comprehensive Study of Antisocial Disorders
    and Behaviors* (editor), 1978.
Psychiatry for the House Officer, 1979.

Basic Intensive Psychotherapy

❋❋❋

William H. Reid, M.D., M.P.H.

Clinical and Research Psychiatrist,
Nebraska Psychiatric Institute of the
University of Nebraska College of Medicine, Omaha

Lecturer in Psychiatry, Northwestern
University School of Medicine, Chicago

Visiting Associate Professor of Psychiatry,
Rush Medical School, Chicago

BRUNNER/MAZEL, Publishers ● New York

Library of Congress Cataloging in Publication Data

Reid, William H. 1945-
    Basic intensive psychotherapy.

    Bibliography: p.
    Includes index.
    1. Psychotherapy. I. Title.
RC480.5.R38   616.8'914   79-24337
ISBN 0-87630-227-4

Published by
BRUNNER/MAZEL, INC.
19 Union Square
New York, New York 10003

MANUFACTURED IN THE UNITED STATES OF AMERICA

To my students

PREFACE

✦✦✦

This book represents an effort to update and clarify the practical and technical aspects of intensive psychotherapy for the beginning therapist. The kind of therapy addressed herein as "intensive," "process," or "insight-oriented" is taken to mean psychotherapeutic treatment of a primarily verbal nature which takes place between a psychotherapist (medical or nonmedical) and an individual adult patient over a prolonged period of time, generally several months or years. A variety of psychotherapeutic approaches are compatible with the basic principles discussed in the pages to follow.

The book assumes a psychodynamic approach to therapy rather than a purely symptom-oriented one. This in turn implies the existence of certain psychological characteristics, including some representational form of emotional *energy,* one or more systems of filters or barriers for the raw energy (*defenses*), *conflicts* between the energy and the defenses and between the self and the environment, motivation for change, resistance to change, and the formation of special kinds of therapeutic alliance. Important to an understanding of the treatment concepts addressed later is the fact that most of these characteristics are essentially unavailable to the patient for ordinary observation or modification. Indeed, the bulk of psychic phenomena and their precursors can be described as *unconscious*.

The text does not directly address itself to crisis intervention, supportive therapy, counseling, or any of a variety of (often very helpful) modes of treatment which are primarily designed for symptom alleviation. Further, the reader will not find on these pages extensive discussions of theoretical bases for the practical guidelines presented or exhaustive information concerning diagnosis. These subjects, which are important to the overall professional education of every psychotherapeutic clinician, should be examined elsewhere in the potential therapist's library, course work, and supervised experience.

Except for brevity and simplicity of approach, likeness may be drawn between this book and some other introductory psychotherapy texts. It is, by design, similar to Kenneth Colby's *A Primer for Psychotherapists*.* Dr. Colby's pithy, practical, understandable work was of inestimable value to young psychotherapists, including the author, as a gentle but thorough and unapologetic introduction to clinical work. It is hoped that this volume will contribute to that tradition.

W. H. R.

Omaha, Sept., 1979

---

* Colby, K. M.: *A Primer for Psychotherapists*, New York: Ronald Press, 1951.

ACKNOWLEDGMENTS

❖❖

Students from various stages of training in psychotherapy have been of great help in the writing of this book. It was originally conceived to meet elementary teaching needs, and matured with much appreciated feedback from psychotherapists in Chicago and Omaha. Thanks are also due Marilyn Pittillo, who ably prepared all drafts and the final manuscript.

CONTENTS

Basic Intensive Psychotherapy

CHAPTER 1

****

Principles and Goals

****

❖❖❖

Among the many definitions of mental health is Freud's now famous statement "To be able to love and to be able to work." Intensive psychotherapy is aimed at allowing certain kinds of patients who do not enjoy this kind of mental health to move from a state of chronic inability "to love" or "to work" efficiently and effectively to one which is more nearly "healthy," symptom-free, and consistent with the emotional and social needs of the individual and his environment.

The methods described in this volume which address this task are sometimes simple and sometimes quite complex. Taken in parts or as a system—that is, "psychotherapy"—our work must be seen, by any standard and from almost every point of view, as *repair*. The concept of repair, used in this context, is thus to be differentiated from that of support (as a therapeutic end), counseling (education), marked covering of conflictual material, or complete reconstruction (cure).

This repair work, if properly done, should assist the patient in his adaptation to his biological, emotional, and external environments. In addition, it should prepare him for future experiences, both gratifying and frustrating, which will come his way from the world in which he lives and from within himself. While specific symptoms are likely to decrease, even more important is the freeing of emotional energy from inefficient, unsuccessful uses, so that it becomes available for more efficient, effective tasks. These include coping with frustrations and traumata, as well as taking advantage of opportunities for pleasure.

It should be remembered that, in order to be successful, psychotherapeutic repair need not be absolutely complete. It is the rare individual who becomes (or feels) perfect after a course of even the most effective psychotherapy. If the above goals are met in substantial measure, the therapist should feel that he or she has contributed to a successful therapeutic experience in the patient (although this is not usually communicated to the patient in so many words—see Chapter 6).

When considering psychotherapy for a patient, planning its course, and evaluating the patient's progress, certain basic characteristics should be explored. Among these are the strengths and weaknesses of the patient with respect to availability for therapy and potential for a successful outcome. Some of the strengths inherent in most patients are the biological substrate on which the physical and psychological mechanisms of life are laid (constitution), characteristics of the emotional self (ego) which have developed in a relatively healthy fashion (ego strengths), less healthy but still potentially useful adapting mechanisms which serve to prevent worsening of symptoms or further decompensation (neurotic defense mechanism), and the wide variety of supports available within the individual's immediate and extended environments (family, home, job, culture, religion, etc.).

Weaknesses of the organism can be similarly observed, and are opposite sides of the same coins on which the above strengths are found. The biological substrate may have serious deficiencies (e.g., genetic predispositions to illness, congenital defects). Aberrant development of the ego and its derivative psychic structures may have given rise to significant deficits. These in turn may have arisen from traumata of such intensity and chronicity that ego strength is severely lacking in some areas. Emotional mechanisms designed to prevent further decompensation and assist in personal and environmental adaptation may be so ingrained or maladaptive that the symptoms they produce are refractory to treatment. By the same token, the balance between developmental deficit and accompanying defense mechanism may be fragile and unable to tolerate the therapy necessary for its manipulation or for removal of some symptoms. Finally, the external environment may contribute problems—in the form of trauma, frustration, or secondary gain—instead of support for therapeutic change.

Thus, the consideration of psychotherapy as a useful treatment for a given patient is once again seen as a consideration related to repair work. One might think of a potential patient in the same way one might evaluate an automobile for repair, by considering the condition of the engine, the extent of hidden damages, the value or "strengths" of other parts of the automobile, the environment in which it must be used, and the tasks to which it will be put, before deciding upon the nature of the work and committing oneself to it.

THE WISH-DEFENSE SYSTEM

No matter what theoretical base one begins with in considering the source of human behavior (both normal and psychopathological) and the psychodynamic means by which the organism protects itself and adapts to the environment, certain concepts are fairly universal in traditional developmental theory. *Energy* (sometimes vaguely termed "psychic energy" or "tension") is part of the biological substrate of the organism from birth. Although it is important to point out that we are not speaking of a strictly quantifiable entity such as heat or light, the concept of psychic energy, which may fuel both constructive and destructive activity and which may develop and/or be transformed as the human being develops and matures, is a valuable one. Some readers may already be familiar with one or more formal structuralizations of this concept. Others, perhaps from more behavioral schools of developmental thought, may reject it. It is enough to say that the idea of psychic energy or tension is a unifying one and is consistent with both understanding and application of the therapeutic techniques described later.

A second concept, which is also so important as to require that it be presupposed before seriously embarking upon the study and practice of intensive psychotherapeutic techniques, is that of the *unconscious* (or, used as an adjective, unconscious motivation for feelings, thoughts, and behavior). Further, the acceptance of the existence of an unconscious, or unconscious motivation, is not in itself sufficient for our work. The therapist must understand that

(1) the unconscious portion of the psyche is considerably more vast than the conscious portion;

(2) the unconscious portion exerts an (unconscious) influence on almost everything that the individual feels, thinks, or does, *and*

(3) the unconscious is unconscious: Unconscious thoughts, memories, motivations and the like are, under ordinary circumstances, totally unavailable to the person who has them. *This is a major reason for the therapist's presence in the treatment.*

Within the unconscious and generally arising from very early stages of psychological development, the individual has a variety of *wishes* (impulses). Fueled by energy (tension) from biological and early developmental *anlagen*, these impulses continuously strive for gratification. At its most basic level, gratification is represented by the uncontrolled release of tension.

Uncontrolled release of tension or psychic energy, as through the unchecked carrying out of a primitive unconscious impulse, is prevented by one or more *defenses**. Emotional defenses, most of which are unconscious, interact and are organized into a complex defensive system. This system, often said to involve an "ego" and "superego," protects the person in several important ways. It serves to *stop destructive impulses* and allows the containing ("binding") of energy that might harm the individual or give rise to anxiety. The defensive system also *mitigates impulses,* channeling energy under tension into forms and outlets which are internally and externally (and consciously and unconsciously) acceptable to the person. Finally, the defensive system is generally seen as *providing ways in which psychic energy can be used* to further emotional growth, repair developmental deficiencies, and form coping mechanisms that work to increase personal and social effectiveness, while they decrease the anxiety that arose from previous, less effective defenses.

Thus every individual has

> wishes (impulses)

which are unconscious and are fueled by

> tension (energy)

from biological and primitive environmental sources, which is prevented from uncontrolled release by

> defenses

which are organized into a complex

> defensive system.

---

* Note that the term defenses is used here in a general way, and is not limited to the specific concepts which may be found elsewhere in the literature (ego defense, neurotic defense, etc.).

Symptoms are conscious emotional or behavioral manifestations of incompletely successful attempts to cope with external or internal stress. External stress (that is, external to the psyche) may come from a variety of sources, such as one's job, a social interaction, a medical illness, or even the weather. Internal stress which gives rise to symptoms (and which may be precipitated or exacerbated by external stress) is said to be related to conflict.

Conflict is represented by an inefficient relationship between a wish and the defenses which keep it in check and deal with the energy that fuels it (the wish). That is, if the psychic energy which strives for release is not completely discharged (primitive wish gratified/tension discharged) or not successfully bound (dealt with by means of defenses which use psychic energy efficiently and are compatible with the emotional self and the environment), then conflict ("neurotic conflict") is said to exist. Such conflict may lead in turn to symptoms and/or clinically discernible signs.

Conflict may be seen as arising from a primitive imbalance of the relationship of wish to defense or wish to early environmental frustration. This is called "core conflict." Conflict may also be seen as related to an imbalance later in life, even in adulthood, between the more mature emotional self (conscious or unconscious) and the environment. This is "derivative conflict," because it is assumed to be at least partially derived from related core conflict.

The goal of the kind of psychotherapy we shall discuss is not solely—or even mainly—simple reduction of symptoms as usually presented to the therapist. Rather, it is to modify certain important wish-defense relationships so that the defense component is less pathologic (more efficient, more socially and emotionally effective), and more appropriate resolution can take place. The therapist and patient work toward a better balance, and toward the use of defenses which are less energy depleting. Usually this means a decrease in unbound tension, accompanied by a decrease in symptoms and signs.

The therapeutic approach described here is not one which ordinarily addresses very primitive (core) conflict. This task is left to the practice of psychoanalysis. Patients, and sometimes therapists, frequently ask about the relationship between psychoanalysis and psychotherapy, especially when the psychotherapy is of an intensive nature and involves some techniques which are associated with psychoanalysis (e.g., use of a couch, free association, interpretation of dreams, or attention to transference phenomena).

Dewald (1978) has discussed the difference between psychoanalytic psychotherapy, a form of intensive psychotherapy, and formal psychoanalysis, using an analogy which compares the patient to a tree. Neurotic symptoms are represented as occurring in one or more branches of the tree. Psychoanalysis explores the branch and follows it centrally, exploring the trunk, the roots, and all the other branches. Psychoanalytically oriented psychotherapy, however, chooses to explore primarily the branch(es) on which the symptoms occur and those limited portions of the trunk which are important for the nourishment, support, and reinforcement of those symptoms. Other portions of the patient's personality, which may represent ego strengths or relatively stable neurotic defense systems, are left alone. Consistent with our earlier discussion of conflict as a source of symptoms, it may be said that psychoanalysis explores and attempts to resolve core conflict ("roots"), while other forms of intensive therapy find exploration and resolution of derivative conflict ("trunk," "branches") sufficient for their various goals.

Anxiety is a psychophysiological characteristic which is referred to throughout the psychotherapy literature. In this book references to it are general and compatible with several viewpoints regarding its origin, dynamics and purposes. It may be helpful to briefly address one of these viewpoints—the classical analytic one—in an effort to clarify the author's intent at the outset.

Theoretical derivatives of Freud's subjective concept of the "pleasure principle" establish anxiety as an uncomfortable state produced when an influx of stimuli to the psyche is too great to be mastered (bound) or discharged ("automatic" anxiety), or when the ego (see below) perceives a danger that such a trauma might occur ("signal" anxiety). The prototype for situations of automatic anxiety is felt to be the birth process, and it is characteristic of infancy and primitive psychic functioning. Signal anxiety is more characteristic of later development, normal emotional functioning and psychoneurosis. It is important to remember that the stimulus for anxiety can originate either inside or outside the individual, and that much of the process of feeling and dealing with it occurs unconsciously.

Anxiety is a crucial component of normal as well as pathological development. It serves as an internal guide for psychological—and, at its most basic level, perhaps biological—growth through reality testing and other processes. It is also a state which the organism tries to avoid. Awareness of the latter principle, along with the knowledge that our minds may *unconsciously* choose a situation of lesser anxiety over one of more, provides the general basis for an understanding of symptoms, apparently maladaptive behaviors, and the intensive psychotherapy process.

The structural hypothesis is Freud's unifying concept which functionally describes major parts of the psyche. Although adherence to it is not a strict requirement for useful therapy, it is the source for many of the terms used in this book, including *id, ego,* and *superego.*

In classical and neofreudian analytic psychology, the psychic representations of the drives, including all basic wishes (impulses), are said to make up the *id.* Many authors, beginning with Freud, assume that the entire psychic apparatus at birth is comprised of the id, part of which soon gives rise to the ego, and later the superego. Others elaborate more or less on the view of Hartmann that there is an initial diffuse core of precursors from which id and structured ego develop after birth. The drives —usually seen as either aggressive or libidinal—supply general direction for gratification and development, and are the source for energy which the ego uses for adaptation and control of anxiety (see below). *Primary process* is a term used to describe emotional functioning which cannot delay gratification (discharge of impulses), and which is characteristic of the id and the immature ego.

The *ego* is that part of the psyche which deals with the environment, both outer and, once experience has supplied the infant with noninstinctual internal memories and percepts, inner. Thus, the adaptive and defensive ego begins to differentiate from the primitive emotional core as soon as the organism's sensing and processing apparatus are biologically capable of responding to the environment. As ego development progresses, a new, more efficient and psychologically safer means of thinking evolves: *secondary process*. This becomes the dominant mode of functioning for the ego, making it able to delay discharge of impulses and allowing logical, nonmagical thought and behavior. The ego gradually assumes control over the voluntary muscles of the body, organs of perception, information storage (memory) and processing (thinking), and feelings. It acts to block unacceptable impulses from the id, to channel them into more acceptable outlets (e.g., with ego defenses), and to turn some of the energy from those impulses to the individual's advantage (e.g., change unchecked rage into useful competitiveness). The ego uses the energy of the id to master it and the environment, toward the aims of survival and safe gratification (pleasure).

The *superego* generally corresponds to the concepts of conscience, morality and ideals. Although some analysts (notably Klein et al.) feel that this part of the psychic apparatus begins to form during the first year of life, most agree that it arises essentially out of the resolution of the oedipus complex, with concomitant internalization of clear, parentally-based rules of emotional survival in the child's environment of interpersonal relations. This occurs at age five or six in most children, and becomes fairly well established after more social interaction has taken place, usually by the end of so-called "latency" (around 11 or 12). A sense of morality is thenceforth felt by the person as coming primarily from within rather than from external sanctions of the environment.

THE THERAPEUTIC PROCESS

Our method for modifying the wish-defense balance which has resulted in conflict within the patient involves two primary on-going goals. First, the patient's own emotional makeup and defense system, as applicable to the therapy, is to be made clear to him or her. This accomplished primarily by the therapist's clarifying these for himself, using methods that will be made clear later, and then communicating this information to the patient in appropriate ways.

Concurrently with work toward the first goal, that of insight, the patient is prepared for what he will find in the therapy. The *observing* part of the patient, a part which may be seen as the healthy portion of the patient which allies itself with the therapeutic effort, is carefully prepared for the discoveries of unconscious feelings or motivations which lie ahead. The patient is also made ready to make changes in his behavior, based upon concomitant changes in various levels of the psyche.

The ability to use this new information in a lasting, meaningful way depends upon more than intellectual awareness. The patient must accept what he discovers about himself with conviction, so that it becomes, through a continuous process of "working through," truly a new part of his self and a tool for more effective adaptation to his internal and external environments.

All of the above imply an ongoing *process*. Intensive psychotherapy must take place bit by bit, since the repetition of the cycle of preparation of the patient, observation or interpretation, working through, and acceptance with conviction often takes considerable time. During this process, several areas of exploration or concern may be involved in the therapy at once, each at varying stages of resolution. At times the focus will be on one or another of these, while the others will be—far from quiescent—in phases of preparation or working through.

The therapeutic process takes place within the *therapeutic relationship* (therapeutic alliance, working alliance). *Transference* is the relationship that occurs when the patient—primarily unconsciously and with unconscious motivation—perceives the therapist with feelings that are related to (and often identical to) those felt toward significant figures of his early childhood, one or both parents for example. True transference will form in intensive psychotherapy and is important for the clarification of psychodynamics. It is also often of use in strengthening the psychotherapist's positive influences on the patient; however, a very intense transference is unusual in this kind of therapy and is generally not to be encouraged. In intensive therapy, as opposed to psychoanalysis, the transference is not allowed to fully mature and is not completely explored (analyzed). Similarly, as described in the "tree" analogy above, such things as early childhood and primitive characteristics of dreams are not exhaustively investigated.

A final basic concept, one which appears in many guises throughout the therapeutic process, is that of *resistance* to the therapy. From before the patient comes to treatment, at which time resistances are usually greater than motivation for change, some parts of him work for retention of inefficient but familiar coping mechanisms. One may see an analogy in the image of a person marooned on a barren but habitable island. He may know that the mainland—or at least a more livable island—exists somewhere beyond the horizon; however, that way is, for him, uncharted. It is difficult to abandon the relative safety of even the most uncomfortable abode.

Resistances are most often seen as reluctance to see or accept some bit of unconscious material which threatens to become uncovered. Some are seemingly minor, as resistance to the idea that being late for appointments may represent passive aggression. Others, including the transference itself, are more obviously complex. All can, with some exploration, be seen to operate against the overall therapeutic process and dissolution of neurotic conflict. The concepts of transference and resistance are more fully explored in Chapter 5.

CHAPTER 2

+++

The Participants: Therapist and Patient

+++

****

THE THERAPIST

Since most of the following pages will be devoted to discussion of the patient, let us begin with a description of the characteristics, training, and tasks of the therapist.

The therapist should have—and the patient has a right to expect of him—a number of basic qualities. A knowledge of normal and pathological human development, defensive systems, and behavior is of course essential. Given that knowledge, the transition from academic to clinical expertise is begun when the therapist acquires comprehensive knowledge of psychotherapeutic technique. "Hands-on" experience with the technical and interpersonal aspects of the practice of psychotherapy is a third requirement. Finally, intimate knowledge of one's own emotional makeup and mastery of many of the characteristics which might interfere with the intensive treatment of others are imperative for the development of the mature professional.

Knowledge of normal development, psychopathology, and treatment technique can be obtained from a variety of sources. Books, seminars, and observation may all be useful.

Clinical experience should be obtained over a period of several years, with graduated amounts of responsibility taken by the student therapist. At the beginning of training, it may be best for patients to be carefully chosen for the therapist and for supervision to be quite close, perhaps by observation or video-tape. Later, even the experienced therapist may wish to obtain supervision or consultation in difficult cases. Besides experience in psychodynamic psychotherapy, previous work in other forms of psychotherapy, counseling, medical or nursing practice, and the like may also be helpful as parts of one's clinical foundation.

An intimate knowledge of oneself implies sufficient understanding of one's emotional strengths and vulnerabilities to allow the therapist to retain an objective helping posture during intimate, often highly stressful contact with the patient. It is clear that one of the best ways to attain such a state is through personal psychotherapy or psychoanalysis. Indeed, the more intensive the therapy that one plans to practice, the more personal exploratory psychotherapy is to be recommended for the potential therapist.

The psychotherapy or psychoanalysis which is recommended for the protection of the therapist and enhancement of his craft cannot be entered into solely for the purpose of "becoming a better therapist." Personal exploration to this end is often useful in therapist-centered supervision; however, one's own psychotherapy should be undertaken with the idea of becoming a patient. The therapist's treatment, whether psychodynamic psychotherapy or training psychoanalysis, is thus no less therapy—and no less repair work—than is that of his patients.

Good psychotherapists may come from many backgrounds and disciplines. Some of these prepare one better than do others. I shall mention psychology, medicine, social work, and nursing, each of which has advantages and disadvantages for the development of the mature therapist.

The clinical psychologist ordinarily comes to his practicum in intensive psychotherapy with a background of education and perhaps an internship with clinical experience. He or she may have had considerable exposure to the theory and technique of other kinds of therapy. This background, and the teachers who have supplied it, can be either helpful or discouraging to the psychotherapy student.

The psychiatrist receives his psychotherapy training during residency. He or she has had a medical background rich in clinical experience but full of techniques and therapeutic models which must to some extent be unlearned. A medical background can be invaluable, instilling a sense of professional ethics and responsibility which will be useful throughout the therapist's career. In addition, there are services which the psychiatrist can offer to his patient which are unavailable to other psychotherapists. These include prescription of medications, some understanding of complex medical problems, and some foundation for the differentiation of serious physiologic conditions from functional symptoms related to the course of therapy or to the therapist-patient relationship.

Persons from nondoctoral backgrounds such as clinical social work and psychiatric nursing often become excellent therapists. Although the lack of a doctorate degree sometimes stands in the way of licensing or professional recognition, such people often come from a background of caring and intimacy with their patients/clients. Indeed, their lack of some of the "programming" of the clinical psychologist and psychiatrist may allow productive work with patients for whom intensive psychotherapy might otherwise be unavailable.

Virtually all individuals from the above disciplines require specialized training and supervised experience in long-term psychotherapy before competence can be expected. This does not mean that such persons are not already equipped to provide quality mental health care to clients with a variety of emotional, social, and medical difficulties; however, the addition of process-oriented insight psychotherapy to one's clinical armamentarium requires some specific commitment to the treatment modality discussed in these pages.

The practice of psychotherapy requires maturity of education and of spirit. A 23-year-old social worker may need several years of post-training experience, preferably with supervision, before becoming a confident therapist. By the same token, a 27-year-old physician is a very new professional, an adolescent in a sense, who may need to gain much personal and clinical experience before becoming comfortable with unsupervised psychotherapy.

In intensive therapy the therapist will encounter feelings and experiences related to, but quantitatively far different from, others in his or her clinical career. In the beginning, the wish to cure one's patient, to be accepted by him, and to be praised by peers and mentors is present in all of us. These must be tempered by the reality of what can be accomplished in the setting offered, and by what is in the best interests of the patient.

Later in the treatment these wishes—often related to the phenomenon of countertransference (the therapist's reaction to the patient as if he were an important figure from the past)— appear in the therapist as various kinds of strong feelings. If these are not recognized and contained or otherwise dealt with, the treatment will be contaminated. The patient's therapeutic needs, which are the legitimate center of attention during treatment sessions, may then take a back seat, consciously or unconsciously, to the needs of the therapist.

The therapist is human. He or she is entitled to gratification for his efforts. If gratification is not allowed to come from the patient, from whom most other helping professionals derive much of their personal reward, then where can it be sought?

One prominent analyst said that the only reward *from the patient* to which the psychotherapist is truly entitled is his fee. This stance is a bit too strenuous for most of us, but the implication is clear. If one wishes to enjoy his profession, to continue it for a number of years and to avoid symptoms of chronic emotional drain or depression, then internal and external resources independent of one's patients must be actively cultivated. Personal psychotherapy can increase one's ability to recognize his own deservedness and to reward himself appropriately. Just as important is the seeking out of relationships among family and friends, as well as participation in peer activities such as professional associations and study groups.

Beginning therapists who have had experience with some form of patient responsibility in the past can readily understand the need to appraise, and sometimes temper, feelings of responsibility in long-term intensive relationships. It is not in the patient's interest for the psychotherapist to take over his work. Attempts to do so (e.g., to force some behavioral change) are generally related to feelings of omnipotence, misplaced guilt, or other countertransference manifestations in the clinician.

Is the therapy, then, a sterile experience from the therapist's point of view, comparable to an operating room in which the patient is laid open to efficient but emotionless intervention? Of course not. The era of the "blank screen" therapist, if it was ever with us, is well past. Although the therapist is not expected to bare himself, to explore his own problems with the patient, or to usurp the patient's session, he may share the *reality* of the treatment setting. Commenting on a loud noise outside the office, mentioning street repair which curtails parking near the clinic, and the like are appropriate and help the patient to see one as real. Similarly, chuckling at a humorous statement or responding appropriately to a sad one can, if not the result of destructive countertransference, facilitate the treatment process and make life more bearable for therapist and patient alike. All of these are signs of genuineness, empathy and respect.

Throughout the pages to follow we will see examples of the therapist's position in the therapeutic relationship and process. As will be shown, there is always a balance of *therapist as real person* and *therapist as transference object*. Both are necessary and both must be understood and properly used in order to eventually effect a good treatment response.

THE PATIENT

In his 1951 book, *A Primer for Psychotherapists*, Dr. Kenneth Colby asked the question, "Who comes to therapy?" He stated that most patients who come to therapy as a result of their own motivation—that is, their own emotional discomfort— come from the middle and upper socioeconomic classes. To some extent, this is true today. Although mental health care is now available to millions of persons for whom it was inaccessible 20 years ago, the social strata of most patients who request process psychotherapy remain about the same.

A number of other characteristics are more important, however, in determining what kind of patient seeks psychotherapeutic treatment. Persons who are already somewhat introspective and who have sufficient insight to wonder about reasons *within themselves* for discomfort or other difficulties are likely to consider ways of exploring the self as potentially productive and symptom-reducing. These are frequently people who are already accustomed to using verbal communication as a means of problem-solving.

Although the beginning psychotherapist may choose his patients for specific characteristics of verbal ability, "psychological-mindedness" and the like, as one gains experience it becomes apparent that many people once considered inappropriate for therapy are today able to explore the idea. As access to mental health care broadens, socioeconomic status *per se* becomes less relevant. Some individuals who often express themselves nonverbally are found to be insightful and receptive to the idea that verbal psychotherapy can be of assistance.

The source of the prospective patient's conflict or other developmental deficiency is another characteristic which predisposes him to choose, not choose, or be unaware of the therapeutic possibilities that intensive treatment may hold. Among the countless nuances of character formation and combinations of defensive systems that exist within the general population, most go unrecognized. This is because they are doing the job for which they were designed; that is, although a trained observer may detect signs of inefficient handling of conflict, the character trait and/or defensive system is "ego-syntonic." One result of this can be an absence of overt psychological symptoms, at least as perceived by the person himself. In such a case, the individual has no reason to consider himself disabled or to seek a form of treatment which requires a large investment of energy, time, and often money.

Even when one is aware that his feelings or behavior is inappropriate (such as in the case of some obsessive characteristics or behavioral deviations which are not experienced as particularly painful), the high degree of motivation necessary to seek help may be absent. In Colby's words, "It is when an important character trait fails in its defensive function or produces some discomforting reality frustration that the patient seeks help." The voluntary patient may thus be seen to possess *prima facie* some ability and motivation for psychotherapeutic work.

Another group of patients come to the psychotherapist because of pressure from some source outside of the individual. Legal sanctions (such as probation), family pressure (as in the case of an adolescent or spouse), or some other reason ("to learn more about myself" or "to become a better therapist") may bring the potential patient to the therapist. Such individuals can, in the right circumstances and with certain psychotherapists, benefit from long-term treatment; however, they are often not to be recommended for the beginning psychotherapist.

The family physician or other professional is a referral source familiar to most of us. Many patients who reach the therapist via his or her recommendation will not be candidates for long-term psychotherapy. Of the remainder, some with the characteristics necessary to potentially benefit from psychotherapy will have had poor referral experiences. The family doctor, internist, clergyman, or even friend who suggests psychotherapeutic treatment must do so with some skill in order to avoid too great a confrontation between the patient and the emotional nature of his symptoms. Similarly, the individual's personal readiness to explore his symptoms with some commitment is important if such a referral is to be more than advice to be taken with a grain of salt or an addendum to the patient's medical chart.

Individuals traditionally considered most suitable for insight-oriented psychotherapy have often been described. In addition to the ability to communicate articulately in an almost exclusively verbal context, intelligence and age have been seen as important characteristics. Although many therapists seek bright, fairly young patients, in the author's experience productive work can be done with people of average intelligence and very often with people of advanced age, provided goals are relatively circumscribed. Studies of outcome of psychotherapeutic treatment have found age, marital status, and social class *per se* to be insignificant.

The person most likely to benefit from therapy, and most likely to be an appropriate case for the beginning psychotherapist, is one who feels distress but whose conflicts (neuroses) do not occupy the major part of his emotional life. Most successful psychotherapy patients have been successful in at least some parts of their personal and social lives as well. They have a previously demonstrated ability to achieve, or at least adapt, within their social and vocational environments (although difficulties in this area may be the very symptoms which need to be addressed in treatment), and they show some competence in the formation of appropriate, lasting attachments to others (object relations). There is a healthy portion of the self (observing ego, ego strength) which can observe and react to that part which is associated with symptoms. This healthy portion is motivated for change and expects the therapy to be helpful.

The patient with good ego strength can be expected to maintain an appropriate balance between his internal and external worlds. He exercises reasonable judgment and is aware of the consequences of his behavior. He is able to reasonably tolerate reality frustrations which impinge upon his wishes for gratification. His impulse control is good, but not so strict that pleasure is rarely allowed.

The patient who suffers from a severe characterologic disorder (i.e., a disorder which chronically fills most aspects of one's life and which is often ego-syntonic), from a schizophreniform thought disorder, or from a major affective disorder such as disabling depression or hypomania is, in general, not an appropriate candidate for psychotherapy alone. The psychotherapeutic treatment of such patients involves concepts other than those discussed herein; often combinations of medication, residential milieu, and psychotherapy are required.

The potentially successful psychotherapy patient should have a life situation which is not overwhelming or markedly inconsistent with the demands which will be made during the therapeutic process. Emotional energy will be continuously required, and consistency will be almost imperative. A patient who must endure a chaotic living situation, who does not expect to remain in the therapist's geographical area, or who receives little support from the family with which he lives may not be capable of the commitment necessary for treatment success. Similarly, happenings in the patient's life which sap the energy necessary for the therapeutic work may impede progress or cause premature termination. The individual who is engaged in a divorce, experiencing an acute loss, undergoing severe vocational stress, or the like, should be treated supportively until the crisis has passed and a commitment of emotional energy can be made.

In short, both the therapist and the patient are expected to dedicate time and energy to the therapeutic process. All of the parameters mentioned above should be explored, or at least touched upon, during the evaluation sessions that precede the decision to begin intensive psychotherapy.

A word should be added with respect to patients who are probable not destined to benefit from process psychotherapy. In addition to the *caveats* implied above, the therapist should seriously consider some other treatment modality for patients who are of low intelligence and/or whose intellectual activity routinely avoids introspection. Syndromes which include multiple psychosomatic complaints often provide unconscious secondary gain (but are not to be confused with malingering) and may be refractory to insight. Patients whose basic emotional makeup is relatively primitive—for example, those who have difficulty with reality testing, a severely inappropriate self-image, primarily projective or paranoid defense mechanisms, magical thinking, overwhelming dependency, marked narcissism, or a predisposition to acute emotional storms—should be carefully evaluated before therapy is attempted by the beginning psychotherapist. Infantile and impulsive characteristics in persons without redeeming ego strengths represent serious barriers to insight and meaningful change. Finally, persons with physical, educational, or cultural limitations (e.g., speech defects, language difficulties), even in the presence of considerable ego strength, motivation, and intelligence, should probably be avoided by the beginning therapist. Although they may benefit from psychotherapy, as may some persons with other contraindications mentioned, their treatment is best approached by more experienced and/or specialized therapists.

Patient Goals. Given a patient who fits most of the criteria for suitability for reconstructive psychotherapy, what goals and wishes bring him to the therapist's office? Some of the things that make him a candidate for intensive treatment have already contributed to his rejection of other means of symptom alleviation, such as other kinds of therapists, pseudopsychological approaches (e.g., faith healers, lay encounter groups), environmental change (vacations, job changes), and serious acting-out of his internal conflict (marked changes in life-style, self-destructive activity). He has conscious expectations of being helped by means of exploration and understanding, perhaps coupled with support and benign guidance. Partly consciously, but partly unconsciously as well, the potential patient very much hopes that he will change without experiencing too much loss of his present support systems. That is, he hopes for a productive experience but one whose anxiety and work are tolerable.

Unconsciously, there is a wish for change to occur passively, with the major effort being expended by the therapist and the patient being a recipient of succor. The patient (almost necessarily) has endowed the therapist with qualities of omnipotence. This fantasy power can be, and will be, perceived as both benevolent and dangerous. Unconscious wishes to achieve lasting acceptance and love from the therapist, to be found "special" in a way, may be accompanied by feelings of anxiety and a need to protect oneself from too much openness and vulnerability. Thus, the patient may show his mettle by means of overt or covert competition, may test the therapist's trustworthiness and the strength of the therapeutic alliance by acting out, or may try to control the intimacy of the relationship in a variety of ways (see Chapter 5). Part of the wish for change to occur without anxiety or loss may be related to another wish, that of maintaining the *status quo* and/or being punished. Fortunately, such wishes often do not become prominent until the therapy is underway and they can be explored along with other issues. The handling of this common form of resistance is discussed in later chapters.

The very nature of the hopes and goals of the patient implies that there are accompanying fears as well. The fear of change has been mentioned. The defensive structures and characteristics which are familiar to the patient should never be underestimated as sources of gratification and hence of resistance to therapy. One should remember that they were created by the psyche for a purpose, that they at least in part accomplish their purpose, and that over the years the patient's entire defensive system has become a consistent, predictable mechanism for adaptation to his internal and external worlds. Using the "desert island" analogy from the last chapter, the island must become intolerable, the unseen mainland must be attractive, and the access to the mainland must be as clear-cut and unambivalent as possible in order to promote optimal therapeutic potential.

Other fears which the patient may voice or which may be hinted at, especially during early sessions, include anxiety about what one may find out, fears that the treatment will be too difficult or that the therapist will not turn out to be as benevolent or omnipotent as expected, concerns that the therapy will somehow cause emotional decompensation, and the like. All of these should be seen as part of a hierarchy of fears, with only the rational-sounding, conscious feelings being expressed early in treatment ("What if I find out I'm not really as manly as I want to be?" or "My family is sort of used to me the way I am."). These overt statements are representative of unexpressed concerns—for example, that the therapist may not follow through with what the patient perceives as a promise to cure him—which, in turn, are related to deep issues of conflict over such things as passivity, dependency, and basic trust.

CHAPTER 3

✠✠

The Therapeutic Setting

✠✠

✤✤✤

PHYSICAL CONDITIONS

Psychotherapy can be accomplished in literally any setting which allows for privacy, quiet, and modest comfort. The institutional or even shabby appearance of some clinics or the absence of plush chairs and soundproof doors need not preclude useful therapy. However, there are a number of considerations which may improve the efficiency of treatment and which contribute to the comfort of both therapist and patient.

The therapist, no matter what his or her level of training or position in the hierarchy of the clinic in which he works, should have his own office. Although it may be shared with another trainee or staff person, it should be a place in which the therapist feels at home. Stark walls can be softened by personal touches of art work and bare floors covered by an inexpensive, sound-deadening carpet. Such decorations may reflect one's particular tastes and needs for comfort—after all, the therapist must spend several hours per day in the office—however, some consideration should be given to avoiding frankly disturbing or seductive items, or those which might overly contribute to some patients' transference fantasies.

The office should be consistent from session to session. In some clinics the move toward egalitarianism and cost effectiveness forces therapists to "sign up" weekly for treatment space, and thus play a form of musical chairs with offices. Since one of the major tasks of the therapist is to help the patient explore feelings from within himself, and even to convince the patient that certain of his feelings are indeed coming from within, a relatively consistent environment is almost imperative in order to avoid confusion. At the same time, the experience of a different office every week or so, with little evidence of the therapist's personal touches, unduly strengthens the patient's resistances before the as yet unformed therapeutic alliance can counter them. After all, if the therapist to whom one has been referred were truly competent (powerful, able to help), wouldn't he at least have an office of his own?

Once one has convinced the clinic administrator or training director that he deserves a bit of consistent office space, hopefully well heated and cooled, not too thin-walled, and not in the midst of major traffic patterns in the building, how does he or she prepare it for the practice of psychotherapy?

Most clinicians would agree that the therapist is entitled to treat himself well. As implied above, one may spend considerable time in the office, sometimes engaged in intensive and draining work. In even the most spartan clinic, the resourceful therapist can find some kind of comfortable chair and bring in a few prints or posters. Small photographs of one's family or friends are not inappropriate, nor are plants and other tasteful touches. Diplomas and certificates may or may not be exhibited (sometimes they are required by law); other medical trappings, such as large scientific charts or models, should be avoided unless one ordinarily uses them with other persons seen in the same office. As mentioned earlier, the therapist should avoid intrusive exhibits or decorations which may confuse the task of determining what material is coming from inside the patient and what has been molded by the environment, including the office milieu. Another consideration has to do with the therapist's need to feel comfortable and competent. Anxiety about such issues is quite normal in new clinicians, but should be discussed with one's supervisor rather than hidden behind pseudoscientific props.

In a related way, the therapist may find himself choosing a particularly large or comfortable chair compared with that of the patient, or may sit behind a desk with a window or bright light behind him. In reality, although the patient has perceptions and wishes with regard to the therapist's authority and superiority, psychotherapy involves alliance more than it involves confrontation. A patient's feeling that he is vulnerable, for example, should come from the process of exploring his own emotions and behavior. It should not be thrust upon him by the office environment.

There are a variety of seating (or reclining) arrangements which are conducive to insight-oriented psychotherapy. The most common today is some variation of a setting in which therapist and patient face each other. This may involve the patient sitting in a chair beside the therapist's desk, or both patient and therapist sitting in similar chairs, perhaps with a low table between them. There should be a somewhat relaxed air and an angle of view which allows both the patient and the therapist to either look directly at the other or avert their gaze from time to time. The distance between therapist and patient should be small enough to allow for easy conversation but not so slight as to make some patients uncomfortable. One should consider having several chairs in the room, so that the patient can have the option of choosing distance, seating arrangement, etc. (choices which can be discussed with the patient at an appropriate time).

The use of a couch by non-psychoanalytic psychotherapists has become uncommon in recent years. There are a number of issues which the psychotherapist should consider before deciding whether or not to ask his patient to recline. First, some patients should not be treated other than face to face. These are persons who have a difficulty with their grasp on reality (such as schizophrenic patients), whose dependency needs are such that not seeing the therapist might constitute an intolerable deprivation, or who have so much seductive component to their current psychopathology that reclining is apt to produce more difficulty than benefit.

From the early days of psychoanalysis, therapists have realized that "indirect" treatment (i.e., treatment which does not involve regular face to face sessions) is less draining upon the therapist. Efforts to guard facial expression and nonverbal communication can sap one's energy and, especially for the beginning therapist, can contribute to the therapist's anxiety and countertransference. It may be remembered that psychotherapy is a treatment which involves the translation of feelings into words, and it is not necessary to face the person with whom one is having a conversation.

Finally, the use of indirect therapy often contributes to the efficiency of the therapeutic process. By removing certain reality cues involved in therapist-patient communication, the patient is encouraged to reach into his own memory and imagination for material. In addition, the patient may be more physically comfortable and, with the therapist out of sight, may feel more free to relax and settle into the work at hand.

The use of a couch (or, more common today, an ordinary sofa which can be used for a variety of seating arrangements as well as the patient's reclining) should not be considered definitive of psychoanalysis, just as psychoanalysis can be carried out without the use of a couch. At the same time, if the patient expresses some confusion as to whether he is beginning psychotherapy or psychoanalysis, the therapist should verbalize, in an educational way, the fact that he is not an analyst and that the therapy, although it may use a number of useful psychoanalytic techniques and principles, is not psychoanalysis.

The use or nonuse of indirect therapeutic technique should never be allowed to interfere with more important aspects of the treatment. While it may be valuable for the psychotherapy student to experience the use of some form of indirect therapy (whether using a couch or, more common in most clinics, having the patient's chair face away from the therapist) with at least one patient during his training, objections to this from patient, therapist, or even supervisor should be honored. The therapist is not there to force the patient to lie down or to imply that "unless you do it my way I can't guarantee the result." Rather, after initial evaluation sessions have taken place face to face, with some discussion of the therapist's techniques (see Chapter 4), the therapist might say: "As I mentioned, working with you facing away from me (or reclining on the sofa) may have some advantages for us. Unless you would prefer otherwise, we'll begin next time with your chair facing away from the desk (or with you reclining)". Reluctance on the part of the patient should be met with understanding and exploration, just as should any other feelings that are brought to the interviews, and no great emphasis placed upon the patient's choice one way or the other. Similarly, the patient's wishes to change position later in the treatment should be honored and then explored.

TIME AND SCHEDULING

Just as consistency is necessary in the physical setting of psychotherapy, so should appointments be scheduled at regular intervals and for consistent durations. Some kinds of insight-oriented therapy can be done with weekly sessions. Most patients and most therapeutic goals discussed here, however, will require two or more sessions per week. In this way, the momentum of therapy is preserved and the important therapeutic alliance develops more fully. Sessions are usually spaced through the week, although in certain circumstances they may be grouped over several consecutive days. At the beginning of therapy, during those sessions partially devoted to education of the patient and clarification of procedural issues, the schedule (along with other arrangements and "rules" of the treatment) should be clearly delineated.

The length of sessions is usually best set at something under one hour. If less than 45 minutes, there may be some difficulty because of the time required for the patient to move into and out of the sometimes intensive intra-session material. Times of more than one hour tend to be tiring for both patient and therapist and have no particular advantage. Such long, or even "marathon" sessions may be appropriate in crisis intervention settings, but are not generally useful in ongoing psychotherapy. A clear understanding of the usual session length is important from the outset. It should be part of the consistency of the treatment process and thus relatively inflexible. In this way, deviations from the norm can easily be spotted and earmarked for exploration.

Some years ago virtually all psychotherapists allowed for a period of rest between sessions (thus the "50-minute hour"). During this time one can relax briefly, jot down a few notes, return telephone calls or prepare for the next patient. In the past decade many therapists have begun to schedule hours "back to back," with no break in between. Although this allows more patients to be seen in a given period, and perhaps allows the therapist to take longer breaks every two or three hours, the author's preference is for the more traditional schedule.

GENERAL BEHAVIOR OF PATIENT AND THERAPIST

Most of the progress made toward change in psychotherapy is based upon the patient's translating thoughts, feelings, and impulses into words and verbal affect that can be understood by both therapist and patient. The office setting and time and scheduling considerations mentioned earlier set the stage for this to happen over a period of time; however, the most important participants are the therapist and patient themselves.

The *fundamental rule** for the patient is that he or she is asked —even required—to verbalize thoughts and feelings freely, just senseless. In future pages we will see how the patient's work moves back and forth between the reporting of this intrapsychic as they come to mind. This may mean expressing material which is pleasant, unpleasant, seemingly irrelevant, or even seemingly material and its interpretation (or assimilation of the therapist's

---

* The fundamental rule is never fully observed by patients. Many therapists prefer merely to communicate to the patient that he is free to express what he wishes, with the assumption that his motivation for change is sufficient motivation for participation.

interpretations). The therapist's verbalizations are all on the side of the patient's healthy self and observing ego, and as such are designed to assist the patient in both of these tasks.

Besides talking, other characteristics of the patient's behavior may be important as communications. The most prominent of these is *affect*. The feelings (sadness, anger, joy, conviction) with which a patient says something, as well as his physical demeanor, give the therapist some idea of the emotional status that the words reflect. The therapist's awareness of nonverbal communication is especially important (e.g., the patient sitting with arms and legs folded in a "closed" manner; a repeated cough in a healthy patient; or a patient who tracks mud into the therapist's office).

Another important nonverbal behavior of the patient, reflective of resistance but interpretable only if the previously mentioned scheduling consistency is adhered to, has to do with missed sessions and lateness. Especially after the first several sessions have passed, missing a regularly scheduled session is an occurrence that must be explored. When there seems good reason to have missed a session (e.g., weather, illness) or when only one session has been missed, one may not choose to place undue weight upon it; however, when scheduling has been agreed to in advance and more than one session is missed, a search for resistance is in order. Also, no matter what the cause, skipped sessions give rise to feelings in the patient—loss, rejection, guilt or others—which should be expressed and explored.

Lateness carries many of the same connotations. Such things as hostility or anxiety, generated by material in past sessions or by unconscious material which threatens to become conscious, may be at work. By the same token, requests by the patient to extend the hour, or to meet with the therapist at unscheduled times, should be explored. Ordinarily, the patient should gently but firmly be encouraged to discuss whatever issue is at hand during the regularly scheduled times and, depending upon the stage of therapy, to explore the feelings underlying his request for extra time.

THE TECHNICAL AGREEMENT

The basic technical concepts, goals, and rules which have been discussed in this and the previous chapter relate to the idea of a therapeutic agreement or contract between patient and therapist. During the first few sessions of treatment, this mutual agreement should be outlined by the therapist and communicated in such a way that there is little opportunity for misunderstanding. Issues which should be addressed include what kind of treatment the therapist recommends for this particular patient, the ways in which he suggests that the two of them carry out those recommendations, and realistic predictions as to outcome. The latter item, "realistic predictions," should not be confused with promises of cure or other expressed or implied guarantees. Rather, the patient has a right to some estimate from the therapist of what will take place and to a discussion of the difference between realistic and magical expectations. Many parts of the therapeutic contract will be only superficially accepted at the time of initial interviews; however, when these same issues are brought up later in therapy (as they almost surely will be), they can be accurately identified as related to feelings within the patient rather than to lack of initial information.

Part of the therapeutic agreement includes promises made by the therapist. These are promises which, he is fairly certain, can be kept. Included are such things as the scheduling of a consistent appointment time, agreeing to notify the patient in advance (if possible) if one is unable to keep an appointment, and the implication that the therapist will be available to the patient for a reasonable length of time. The psychiatric resident who will be rotating to another service within a few months, for example, must not give his new patient the impression that he will be available for a longer period.

At this time the patient makes promises as well. He or she enters into an agreement to keep the appointments, to do the therapeutic work, and to be responsible for the fees incurred.

Fees. Monetary agreements may be handled in a number of ways. In some clinics patients are seen without regard to ability to pay; in others much of the fee is underwritten by some form of third party payment; finally, there is the situation in which the individual is personally responsible for the entire bill. Although the author does not conform to the once-held belief that a significant out-of-pocket payment is "part of the therapy," the financial arrangements must be understood by both parties. When the patient is responsible for payment, money easily becomes a symbolic part of the therapeutic process. If an insurance company pays the bill, the therapist may find that his dealings with the third party payer can become a complex part of the patient's resistance (and an administrative headache). One partial solution is to require that the patient pay his or her bill and then receive reimbursement from the insurance company, rather than having the therapist paid by "assignment." Even in the subsidized clinic, which can accept patients solely on the basis of therapeutic suitability and without regard to socioeconomic status, issues of responsibility, courtesy and resistance can become quite complex. A patient who frequently misses appointments, for example, may rationalize such behavior with a statement such as, "Well, the weather was bad and I knew it wouldn't cost me anything to skip the appointment."

In the last analysis, overall costs to the patient are more important than fees *per se*. The major costs are the same as the major parts of the patient's side of the therapeutic agreement. Most draining is the tremendous *energy* that he or she will spend learning, exploring, working through, and changing over the ensuing months or years. For many patients the *time* invested is significant (e.g., a professional person who may spend several hours a week in sessions or commuting to them, and away from his business or practice). The psychotherapist's fee is often among the least of the costs to the patient in the long run.

Should the patient be charged for missed sessions? It at all possible within the administrative framework in which the therapist finds himself, some charge should be made for skipped appointments. In the best of all clinical worlds, the patient is charged identically whether he is in the office or not, late or not. Such practice by the therapist is a clear indication that the

patient's hour is truly his and is the patient's responsibility (as is
the therapeutic work itself). It also implies that the therapist's
time is valuable and worthwhile. Most therapists have some sort
of arrangement by which the patient may cancel for certain
reasons or with some advance notice. Cancelled sessions which
are filled by another patient should never be charged to the person who was absent.

The patient cannot charge the therapist for missed appointments, lateness, etc. Thus, the therapist has some responsibility
to keep those appointments, to be on time, and to allow appropriate extra time when he is late. Time spent with the patient
should by and large be uninterrupted, although many clinicians
answer the telephone briefly during sessions. Such interruptions
are kept short, since the time belongs to the patient at hand.
When crises occur with patients other than the one with whom
one is working during a particular session, a decision must be
made by the therapist. If interruption is unavoidable, then
one should convey this to the patient as an uncontrollable
circumstance.

Note-taking. The taking of notes has a number of uses and
implications. Most therapists have some routine for recording and
organizing what takes place during sessions. Whether very brief
(a few key words per hour) or "process" style (a script of the
entire interview), the notes should remind one of the content,
flow, and dynamics of treatment. Both factual material and the
therapist's deductions may be jotted down, often in shorthand
form.

*No method of note-taking should interfere with the flow of
therapy or with the therapist's ability to observe the therapeutic
process.* Continuous writing or other obvious motions of recording
can be distracting to the patient. Just as important, these focus
the therapist's attention on the words of the session rather than
on important psychodynamic events. Excessive note-taking may
indicate a therapist's anxiety in the therapy setting, a resistance
to some part of the task at hand.

Whether and how notes are taken will be noticed by the patient.
No matter what the therapist's method, many associations and

fantasies can result. If one writes copiously, the patient may feel "He's very interested," *or* "I wish he'd stop writing long enough to listen," *or* "I wonder who else will read all those notes he's taking." If one writes little, similar positive and negative thoughts will ensue ("I wonder why he chose to write *that* down," etc.). All of these feelings are grist for the therapeutic mill.

The deciding factors for one's own practice should be related to (1) what works best for the particular therapist, (2) what one's supervisor may recommend, and (3) what the clinic requires in the way of official records. As a general rule, the official record (e.g., hospital chart) should be separate from your private notes and should contain only limited information entered on a need-to-know basis. (See *Confidentiality and Communications,* page 00).

Some therapists use tape recorders or videotape equipment during some or all of their sessions. While this may free the clinician to concentrate on the therapeutic process, it is the rare person who actually listens to the entire tape later. Unless taped sessions are part of a learning or supervisory experience, a few notes from time to time would seem to be less troublesome and obtrusive.

An example of brief notes, followed by a translation of the therapist's "shorthand":

12/22/78—OT-Re week; wish for ↑ sessions. Friend sick, Dr.; Sis's death Thanksg. '76. Dr. for Sis ((tears)). Respons. for kids/exhusb. gone ((M.O.F.)). (Xmas) re Xmas ((M.O.F.)) (Theme: ↓ cared for/left/my Xmas vacation) → accept/ponder/gift fant—both ways—fant re my Xmas and my return. End (Mery Xmas—RTC 2 wks).

Translation: The patient arrived on time (OT) and began with a routine description of her week. At times she wished that she and the therapist could meet more often. A friend is ill and has been seeing a doctor. She is reminded of her sister's illness and death during another holiday season, and becomes tearful as she recalls her sister's pain and the doctor's inability to cure her. Her tone changes to one of matter-of-factness as she talks of her responsibility for her children. Her ex-husband is away and will not see them. The therapist asks about the upcoming Christmas holidays, and the patient talks matter-of-factly of being alone and caring for the kids. The therapist mentions several themes that have been present in much of the conversation today—being cared for, being loved, being left—and wonders aloud whether these in part have to do with his own Christmas vacation and the resulting brief hiatus in treatment. The patient ponders this and responds with fantasies about exchanging gifts with the therapist, wondering what he will be doing, and whether he will return as scheduled. The session ends and the therapist wishes the patient Merry Christmas, reaffirming the return appointment.

Names. Under most circumstances, addressing the patient as Mr. or Ms. is most appropriate. First names should be used only if they will not convey an attitude of familiarity or patronization (e.g., of an older or younger patient). The therapist may often avoid using names in order to observe the patient's own naming without contamination. Whatever one's routine, feelings about it and deviations from it can always be explored.

Gifts from the patient can have many simultaneous meanings, most of which are part of the therapeutic process which is going on at the time of giving or purchase (or making of handmade gifts). Whether or not the therapist chooses to accept the gift, the patient's motives (see sections on Transference and Resistance, Chapter 5) must be discussed. If a gift is handmade, not accepting it may imply more personal rejection than if it is purchased. Expensive gifts should be declined. If the therapist finds himself the recipient of frequent gifts from patients, he should try to determine whether he is conveying messages of seduction, neediness, or threat (see Chapter 6).

The patient who becomes physically ill or is hospitalized should be contacted by the therapist or visited briefly (if in the hospital). In certain cases treatment can be continued in the hospital; however, it is ordinarily best to interrupt therapy until the patient can come to the office.

Major life decisions. In years past, therapists often discouraged their patients from making major decisions (e.g., regarding marriage, divorce, becoming pregnant) until therapy had terminated, on the grounds that strong feelings are often related to transference. Decisions made on such bases were felt to be acting-out, and thus likely not to be in the patient's long-range interest. Today most therapists feel that there is no reason to ban major decisions. In fact, such an ban may be infantilizing and itself a focus for acting-out. It is important, though, that the patient have the opportunity to discuss his or her plans fully, in the light of the transference and other aspects of his emotional state.

Social encounters at which the patient glimpses or meets the therapist may occur, especially in small towns and restricted (e.g., university) environments. Reactions and associations to such situations should always be discussed (see Chapter 5); however, the therapist need not go out of his way to avoid them. The therapist should not accept invitations from patients, nor seek patients out, for example, at parties. If one is aware that a patient is at a particular function, he need not cease being "human," but his behavior should be such that the patient's feelings and privacy are respected.

Confidentiality and Communications. Except in cases of clear danger to self or others, confidentiality must be assured. Information should not be released to anyone, including family or insurance companies, without discussion with the patient and written release. Third party payers often request detailed information; however, a simple statement of diagnosis, time spent and charges is almost always sufficient for payment.

Comments in the clinic chart must be written with confidentiality in mind. Extensive notes should not be placed in the record, which is subject to agency review and subpoena, and is available to many people (including the patient).

Sometimes a patient asks the therapist to communicate with

others on his behalf. Such requests often represent resistance or manipulation (see Chapter 5). The therapist may decide to honor some (e.g., for a brief statement of eligibility for insurance); others (e.g., for a letter of recommendation) should be declined. All hold potential for exploration.

An understanding of the concept of confidentiality and the circumstances under which information will be released should be reached during the first session.

CHAPTER 4

Opening Phases of Treatment

✚✚

THE INITIAL INTERVIEWS

The previous chapters described the many characteristics of patient and therapist that must be considered before long-term therapy becomes a treatment of choice. One to three initial interviews should be allowed for a preliminary evaluation and decision regarding treatment before the patient and therapist commit themselves to such an investment. This time should be used for a relatively formal evaluation procedure, an example of which is described below. In addition, the patient is forming his own impressions, conscious and unconscious, of the therapist. Finally, these early interviews should provide the patient with didactic information as to what psychotherapy is, how his particular therapist works, and what the ground rules of treatment will be.

Although this period is technically different from later sessions, it should be remembered that the therapeutic process starts before the patient even comes to the office. He or she has overcome some resistances and has kept the first appointment. Fantasies and expectations have been formed. The initial meetings with the therapist alter and add to pre-interview feelings, contributing information and structure for the real aspects of therapy, as well as some fuel for fantasy.

With most patients of the type who are recommended for intensive therapy, information-gathering can be spread over more than one session. The evaluation is in some ways similar to the "medical model" in that it should supply an organized body of historical and psychological information; however, the therapist has the luxury of not having to rush. One can listen to the patient without the feeling that an exhaustive differential diagnosis and treatment plan must be completed by the end of the first visit.

One prominent benefit of this approach is that more importance can be attached to feelings than to accuracy. In Freud's early career he was surprised at what he thought to be a very high rate of incest in his patients' childhoods. Later, he found that most of their reports were not factual, but represented important fantasies within the individuals he was treating. This discovery did not, however, alter the importance of such childhood feelings to the elucidation of symptoms and conflict. Without defending either incest or inaccurate records, it can be said that the fantasies and feelings related to a particular statement are often more important than its veracity. Thus, a comment such as, "Everyone is down on me at work. The mail has been late three days in a row. If they'd just give me the chance I'd really show them what I can do," should be heard by the therapist not only as a communication about the patient's real work situation, but also as a possible expression of feelings of being treated unfairly, wishes for acceptance, or defenses against a low self-image.

Presenting Complaint. The therapist should make note of the patient's specific reasons for seeking treatment. These represent real discomforts and are often symbolic of underlying problems. It is not uncommon to later find that the presenting complaints are less important to the patient than some other difficulties, and that the former have been used as an *entree* in order to gain access to the helping environment.

Past History. A careful history of the discomforts or other symptoms which the patient describes is important. When did they seem to begin? Have they been continuous? Intermittent? Getting worse? Why did the patient choose to come and see you at this particular time? What are the patient's feelings as to the source of the symptoms and what might be done about them?

Following the history of the presenting complaint(s), a rather complete psychiatric history should be obtained, including potential associations between the current symptoms and emotional and environmental events in the patient's life. Previous experiences with psychotherapy should be briefly explored at this time, including successes, failures, apparent reasons for terminating, and the like.

Developmental, social, and family histories should be obtained and should be as detailed as a relaxed, permissive interview atmosphere allows. In addition to the query "How and when did your father pass away?", the therapist who is evaluating a patient for intensive treatment would also ask, "How did you feel when your father died?" and "How do you feel about it now?" A brief medical history, including a review of systems, a description of current medical treatment, and a list of medications being taken, should be completed. Many medically trained therapists, especially those in university clinics, may wish or be required to physically examine the patient. While some psychiatrists and psychiatric residents feel strongly about retaining their medical identification, the author recommends that such physical exams be performed by a colleague rather than by the therapist himself.

Dynamic or Diagnostic Formulation. The above information and the experience of eliciting it allow the therapist to arrive at a tentative formulation of the patient's major conflicts and overall personality structure (including his characteristic patterns of coping, relationships, and defense) and of the developmental process which led to his current psychological state. A formal diagnosis need not be made to achieve this; however, such structuring of one's thoughts about the patient acts as a guide for predicting the course of treatment. Should diagnosis be required by the clinic or supervisor, the dynamic formulation of the case may help considerably, and should always be consistent with one's final impression.

At the end of the agreed upon evaluation period, the therapist supplies the patient with a summary of those relevant findings which the patient can utilize and recommendations for their work together. Frank verbalization of one's findings, in a way that is neither frightening nor threatening, need not be upsetting to the patient. Indeed, it implies that such things are not secret or powerful, and that discussing them openly is an appropriate part of the therapy process. This is also true if the therapist has decided not to accept the patient for this kind of treatment. Some examples:

> *Therapist*: "We've spent a couple of hours together now, and you've shared a lot of feelings and information with me. Perhaps we should discuss where to go from here."
>
> *Patient*: "I feel like we're just getting started."
>
> *Therapist*: "I kind of agree. You've described a number of feelings and symptoms that are uncomfortable for you. But there seems to be a great part of you that isn't so affected, a part that could explore some of the reasons for your discomfort and perhaps discover some ways to change it. I would recommend that we continue the therapy on a regular basis, with the understanding that we discussed earlier about commitment and the like."
>
> *Patient*: "It sounds like an awful lot of work, but exciting in a way. And I'm getting tired of feeling the way I do so much of the time."

*   *   *

> *Patient*: "Well, this is the last of those evaluation appointments you wanted me to have. I guess now you know whether all that pain in my back is really in my head."
>
> *Therapist*: "I'm not sure what all of the reasons are for the

> pain. If by 'in your head' you mean imaginary, I don't
> think that at all."
>
> *Patient*: "Oh it hurts all right. And to be honest with you
> I can't see how just talking is going to make it feel any
> better."
>
> *Therapist*: "You've had a good deal of trouble finding any
> relief."
>
> *Patient*: "I don't know what you're saying; if you think I'm
> faking. . ."
>
> *Therapist*: "Not at all. You seem to have been quite honest
> with me and you've certainly followed through with
> your orthopedist's referral."
>
> *Patient*: "Does that mean I'm done here?"
>
> *Therapist*: "I think so, although I'd be happy to talk further
> with you at some future time if you like."

In the first example the therapist encouraged psychotherapy because his evaluation indicated a woman with neurotic symptoms and good ego strength. He was unambivalent in his recommendation, and supportive in that he made it clear that the patient's symptoms were to be seen as somewhat separate from the rest of her "healthy" self. In the second example the initial sessions revealed a man with a strong psychological component to somatic symptomatology. The history of the symptoms and the individual's developmental and social history indicated considerable involvement at a chronic, "personality" level, with significant unconscious secondary gain. The therapist's feeling that the individual would probably not benefit from further sessions, at least not of the process type, was communicated in a non-perjorative manner, in this case probably to the patient's relief.

The evaluation sessions, although in a real sense the beginning of therapy, are not interpretive. The therapist's questions and statements are fairly concrete, giving the patient room to move about and to decrease his or her resistance, while subtly encouraging continued participation, supporting the patient as needed, and setting the stage for the psychotherapeutic process. Such early concreteness and support can be reassuring; however, the therapist's attitude should not be inconsistent with the personal exploration and self-sufficiency that one will expect of the patient later in treatment.

Thus, there are two aims of the initial interviews. The first is a *diagnostic formulation of the patient*. Such a formulation, including clarification of psychodynamics, is essential to the early decisions which must be made at this time. Although the diagnosis and treatment plan are established early, the therapist should occasionally test them against further data which become available as treatment progresses. As one becomes more adept, the probability of major changes having to be made later in treatment (e.g., a shift from intensive psychotherapy to support and medication for a patient whom one discovers to be schizophrenic) will decrease.

The second aim of the initial evaluation sessions is similar, but from the patient's point of view. The patient has the opportunity to briefly *try out psychotherapy* (and the therapist) without considerable commitment of energy and money. He or she begins a process of acclimatization in an atmosphere of support and acceptance. The opportunity for a smooth transition from the pre-therapy state to the stresses and realities of later phases of treatment is thus enhanced.

BEGINNING THERAPY

After the initial evaluation sessions, therapy settles down to the form that it will take for most of the rest of treatment. The patient is expected to supply the bulk of the material for the therapeutic work. This material may come from the patient's current life situation, from his memories of the past, from dreams and fantasies, from the sessions themselves, or from a combination of these.

No matter what the content of the material, or its source, the therapist trains the patient to explore the feelings with which it is associated. Unlike the relatively concrete atmosphere found during the initial sessions, the educational process for the patient now becomes one of experience. We shall explore some common treatment situations of this early phase.

Questions. Material may be presented in the form of questions. At various times the therapist may choose to turn a question back to the patient, to ask the patient to explore its meaning, to deal with it himself, or to remain silent. For the most part, the therapist will want to respond in some way, sometimes with a direct answer, and then suggest that the feelings behind the question be explored. Some examples:

> *Patient*: "The noise outside is terrible. I wonder what they're doing out there?"
> *Therapist*: "They seem to be tearing up the whole street; they've blocked off traffic and everything."
> *Patient*: "Yes, I noticed that when I tried to park in front of the building. Seems like life is full of inconveniences lately. Last week I couldn't get anything to work right..."

Comment: The patient asked a direct question about an obvious characteristic of the environment. The therapist gave a direct answer and the patient proceeded to relate the situation to issues relevant to the therapy.

*   *   *

> *Patient*: "I guess I spend more time than I should wondering about your family, how many children you have and things like that." (pauses)
> *Therapist*: "Um hmm."
> *Patient*: "*Do* you have children, Doctor?" (pauses)
> *Therapist*: "You seem to have a lot of feelings about families and parenting. Might some of them be related to yourself and your own children?"

Comment: This question was related to both the transference and the patient's feelings about herself. Rather than contribute to a resistance by answering the question, the therapist recommended exploring the feelings involved. In this case, the therapist might also have commented on the patient's implied con-

cern that she was "spending more time than she should" on the
subject, as if it somehow might not be proper.

*   *   *

    Patient: "Sometimes it gets me down. All this effort, I
        mean, and the money. What would I do with the extra
        time and money if I weren't in therapy? (pause) I'd
        probably waste it some other way. (hastily) I don't
        mean it's wasted here, but . . . but that's what I said,
        isn't it? I wonder if I'm mad or disappointed or some-
        thing. I sent off for a magic kit once and never got
        it. Wasted the money."

Comment: The patient was using questions for communication and exploration; there was no need for the therapist to
answer. In fact, any answer would have been an interruption
of the patient's associations, which were proceeding nicely.

*   *   *

Silences. There are few situations that cause more anxiety
in the new therapist than the patient's silence. Like the questions
discussed above, silences can have many meanings, often several
at once. There are some situations in which the therapist should
let the patient "stew" for a time. Ordinarily, however, the therapist should respond in a manner consistent with what he or
she feels the silence may mean, as by asking about the patient's
thoughts or feelings, making a tentative observation related to
the material just prior to the silence, or asking a specific question about the material being discussed.

    The therapist does not, however, convey any sense of urgency
or discomfort. He should show that he is as tolerant of this
behavior as he is of any other, that he still adheres to the idea
that it is the patient's responsibility to bring material into the
sessions, and that—most of all—he is interested in the feelings
and meanings associated with the silence.

    Patient: (Silent for the first 30 or 40 seconds of the
        session)

Therapist: "Where shall we begin today?"

Patient: "I don't know. My mind was a blank when I came in."

Therapist: "You were silent. What was in the silence?"

*   *   *

Patient (Finishing a point): ". . . and that was the end of that." (pauses for 15 or 20 seconds)

Therapist: "How did you feel about that conversation with Barry?"

Patient: "I told you—lousy." (silence)

Comment: This patient had two silences within a few minutes. Knowing that she had in the past used silence as a way of acting-out, literally keeping the therapist guessing and interested, the therapist chose to wait several minutes before responding. The session continued:

Patient (after two or three minutes): "I can't think of anything to say . . . help me, will you?"

Therapist: "You'd like for me to participate, to rescue you and express an interest in your feelings."

Patient: "You *are* the doctor, and sometimes I'm in pain."

Therapist: "It sounds like your feelings *are* painful, like the feelings that you experienced with Barry."

Patient: "Damn right. You just won't give a woman any satisfaction, will you. All of you."

Comment: On the one hand, the therapist did not wish to uselessly prolong the patient's discomfort, as might have occurred had he not responded. She would have been encouraged to continue her silence, which might have become a nonverbal fight to see who would "give up" first. By the same token, he did not wish to be seduced into a nonproductive, adversary-like discussion of why the patient should talk, the need for the patient to supply the material for exploration, and the like. His comments were first interpretive, then supportive, but not so much so that the important issue—that of frustration of dependency needs—was avoided. There was a compromise between a heightening of anxiety and alleviation of it, the latter of which would have temporarily gratified the patient's needs and decreased her motivation to further explore relevant feelings.

*   *   *

Patient: "We've only done that once. Well, maybe twice..." (silence for about 30 seconds)

Therapist: "You interrupted yourself when you were recalling how many times you met your female colleague for lunch."

Patient: "I was thinking that it's really been several times, and it would be more if she had accepted every time I wanted to go. Lord, maybe I really am attracted to her like my wife said. But I love my wife, not her."

Comment: The patient interrupted his thoughts with silence in order to prevent his wishes to have an affair from becoming conscious. The therapist, working on the side of the observing ego, kept track of the thought and the patient began to develop insight.

*   *   *

The relatively new patient equates signs of the therapist's attention with evidence of acceptance. Early in treatment the patient may be put off by a lack of response to a question or silence, necessitating some maneuver on the therapist's part to prevent such feelings from becoming larger resistances than necessary. Usually a brief explanation followed by an invitation to the patient to explore the feelings involved is sufficient. Besides the handling of some questions and silences, other examples of therapist behaviors associated with attention and favor, and thus (in the patient's mind) with acceptance, include responses to requests for medication, extra time, or other evidence of concern.

Medications. As part of the initial evaluation and review of the patient's psychiatric history, the therapist should decide within the first few sessions whether and what medications are likely to be necessary during treatment. Many patients who require neuroleptics, including lithium, are not good candidates for intensive psychotherapy by a beginning therapist. Some patients who suffer from severe depression benefit from both antidepressants and insight-oriented therapy; however, the majority of these patients should probably be engaged in more superficial or supportive treatment than is discussed in these pages. Many patients will have alleviated some symptoms with anxiolytics (minor tranquilizers) or sleeping medications before therapy begins.

It is not the therapist's intent to force the patient to give up his coping mechanisms, whether they be behavioral or pharmacologic. If the patient is taking medication when treatment starts, this can be discussed and a recommendation made as to whether it will be necessary, helpful, and/or detrimental to the therapy that is planned. If the therapist is also a physician, he will usually prescribe the medication himself, although there are psychodynamic pros and cons to this practice. For the non-medical therapist, the author feels that the best position to take is that of leaving medication decisions up to the patient and his physician (although *feelings regarding that decision, as well as the drug, should be part of the therapy*). The outside physician should be clearly identified as primarily a supplier of medication, in order to prevent dilution of the therapeutic alliance. By the same token, close communication between physician and therapist, although it may seem to be in the best interests of mutual understanding, should usually be avoided unless the patient's well-being is clearly at stake. This encourages the patient to communicate directly with the therapist, avoids the complexity of having a third person in the treatment arena, and reaffirms the patient's autonomy in the conduct of his affairs.

If the issue of medication comes up later in the therapy, for example with regard to symptoms which have appeared or worsened since treatment began, then the decision is more complex. Although a prescription may be helpful, requests from the patient for drugs very often have to do with issues which are better treated psychotherapeutically. Some examples:

> *Patient*: "This anxiety is getting to be counterproductive. Valium has worked for me in the past; perhaps you could prescribe some."
>
> *Therapist*: "Sounds like you feel overwhelmed."
>
> *Patient*: "Yes. I think a prescription would take the edge off, so that I could settle down and work in therapy."
>
> *Therapist*: "We can talk about your wish for medication, just as we can talk about all feelings. For now, exploring the anxious feelings may be more useful than temporarily suppressing them with Valium."

Comment: The patient was communicating her feelings of anxiety and was trying to be certain that the therapist understood them. She was also expressing her wish for a response to those feelings and testing the strength of the therapeutic agreement to try to avoid medications. Even in the face of the implied bargain ("If you give me some Valium I'll give you good therapy material"), the therapist continued with the methods agreed upon earlier in treatment.

*   *   *

> *Patient*: "My migraines have returned. I know that the therapy uses words instead of pills, but I haven't had time to find a family doctor since moving to town. Could you give me a prescription for Cafergot to tide me over?"
>
> *Therapist*: "I'd prefer not to, especially since I'm not a headache specialist. Perhaps a friend or the local medical society could refer you to someone who could see you without delay."
>
> *Patient*: "I'll try the student health service. It sure hurts sometimes."
>
> *Therapist*: "I understand migraines can be excruciating. Tell me, why do you think they've returned just now?"

Comment: Some therapists would have offered more direct help, such as referral to a specific colleague; others would have avoided discussing the somatic symptom for fear of reinforcing it. In this case, the clinician felt that a compromise was indicated and gave some specific assistance as well as an opportunity to discuss the feelings involved.

* * *

Patient: "Dr. Smith said that she'd give me some sleeping medication if it is okay with you. She asked me to tell you to give her a call and talk with her about it."

Therapist: "The decision for medication is really between you and Dr. Smith. I'd prefer to talk over your feelings with you in person rather than discussing things with her, although I'd be happy to give you a brief note stating that I see no psychological contraindication to whatever your decision might be."

Patient: "You would? I guess that's not necessary right now—I've slept pretty well the last couple of nights—but I'll keep it in mind."

Comment: This therapist was not a medical doctor but the principles involved apply to psychiatrists as well. The therapist chose not to become involved in transactions with an outside physician since these might confuse issues of therapy and encourage fantasies in this particular patient of surreptitious, behind-the-back dealings. He expressed support by making it clear that the patient's feelings are of primary importance in the sessions and by offering to write a brief note. The patient's response indicated that this show of concern was probably more important than the prescription itself.

* * *

Other requests which have to do with testing the therapist's attention, acceptance, dedication or whether he meant what he said at some earlier time, cover such a wide range that it is impossible to treat them completely here. Some common examples involve questions related to the patient's family and to the scheduling and duration of sessions:

> *Patient* (at first evaluation session): "My wife wanted to talk to you too."
>
> *Therapist*: "How do you feel about that?"
>
> *Patient*: "It's okay with me. She can tell you a lot about me."
>
> *Therapist*: "Since you're the one who came to see me, our work will be between the two of us. She may be wondering what all this will be like for her and for your marriage, however. If you wish, the three of us can talk a bit today."
>
> *Patient* (relieved): "That sounds reasonable."

Comment: The therapist did not wish to gather information about this patient from his wife, nor to convey an impression that he, she, and the patient were fighting the patient's problem together. The therapist was aware, however, that support of the patient at home would be important to the therapy, and agreed to see her with the patient to answer general questions about the treatment. He was also aware that by actually seeing the therapist and the therapy setting, the patient's wife would have a real image upon which to organize her feelings as the husband's therapy progressed. The patient's relief was primarily related to the assurance that he was in individual, not family therapy, and that any such discussions would be held in his presence.

*   *   *

> *Patient* (at sixth session): "My wife says that therapy isn't helping. Unless I change by Christmas she's going to leave. She said she'd talk with you if you have time. How about it?"
>
> *Therapist*: "Sounds like you're feeling a lot of pressure."
>
> *Patient*: "I sure am! I'm doing my best to change, but it doesn't happen overnight. She wants everything too fast. She even wants part of you."

Therapist: "What do you think of that?"

Patient: "You're *my* therapist; I'm the one in therapy. I told her you would do what was best for us, even see the two of us together."

Therapist: "It doesn't sound like that's a good idea right now. As you point out, it's your therapy. Tell me more about the pressure you're feeling."

Comment: The therapist perceived, and chose not to participate in, struggles for power within the patient's family. He focused on the therapy as the patient's alone, making note of some early signs that he (the therapist) either was being seen as somewhat omnipotent or was being flattered for some purpose.

* * *

Patient's spouse (by telephone): "Doctor, I'm sorry to trouble you but I feel you should know that Pat is (doing better, doing worse, not taking prescribed medications)."

Therapist: "I can understand your concern; however, it is my agreement with Pat that we work alone, in the sessions scheduled. I'll mention your call, and in the meantime perhaps your talking with Pat would help clarify things."

Spouse: "Oh, please don't say I called. That would make things worse."

Therapist: "I understand your feelings, but I'll need to mention the call."

Comment: Family members are often anxious about the patient's progress, his potential change, and what goes on in the sessions. Calls such as the above should be politely cut short and mentioned to the patient. Under ordinary circumstances, no unrequested information should be accepted from anyone but the patient, even when it may seem to be in the patient's best interest.

There are, of course, many patients whose best treatment includes information from and/or participation of the family.

The reader should be aware of individual needs; however, these case examples apply to most patients for whom intensive therapy is the treatment of choice for the beginning therapist.

*   *   *

> *Patient*: "After my sister left home, things really changed."
>
> *Therapist*: "I'm afraid our time is up for today. Why don't we start with that next time."
>
> *Patient* (continuing): "Okay. I got my own room, but I also began to get the hassling and pressure of being the oldest daughter. Do you have any idea how that feels?"
>
> *Therapist* (rising): "Sounds like quite a change."

Comment: Although a sentence or two in parting is often appropriate (and often contains material which can be discussed at the next meeting), frequent requests for extra time at the end of the interview should be explored rather than passively granted.

*   *   *

> *Patient* (by telephone): "Jerry and I had another argument and I'm really upset. Do you have time to see me tomorrow instead of Friday?"
>
> *Therapist*: "You do sound upset. It might be better, though, if you try to deal with things and come in at the regular time on Friday."

Comment: The therapist, with considerable knowledge of this patient's background, felt that the benefits of encouraging self-sufficiency and letting things cool off outweighed any need for crisis intervention. Consistency, with the expectation that the patient could cope between sessions and the promise that the therapist would be there for appointments that were scheduled, had a variety of advantages in this case.

*   *   *

> *Patient*: "Because of the Christmas rush we are all being asked to work late on Tuesday. Could our meeting next week be on Monday instead?"

Therapist: "I think so. How does 10:30 sound?"

Comment: The therapist, seeing no indication of serious resistance, allowed a reasonable change in schedule. The patient requested the change as soon as she knew about her work problem, rather than calling at the last minute. The treatment was not interrupted and the patient's job—part of the real world in which she lived—was allowed for.

*   *   *

Flexibility in scheduling, as in other areas of technique, may vary from therapist to therapist. Consistency of individual approach and concern for the therapeutic process are more important than one's particular technical preferences.

CHAPTER 5

※·※

The Middle Phase

※·※

The early part of the middle phase of therapy overlaps with the beginning phase just discussed. By this time, the patient's commitment to therapy is mutually understood, the therapeutic alliance is becoming firm and transference is developing, and the therapist has begun to share with the patient his interpretations of the patient's comments and behavior.

In the middle phase work is done on and with the ego. The therapist and patient are engaged in the reduction of derivative neurotic conflict and the reshaping of coping (defense) mechanisms, in order to allow more efficient use of emotional energy in both environmental adaptation and internal defense. Symptoms, which by and large serve to protect the conscious self from experiencing these conflicts, will come to have far less psychic use once they (the conflicts) are resolved, at least partially, although some behaviors may remain at the patient's choice or as habit patterns.

As stated earlier, this form of psychotherapy deals primarily

with derivative conflict, that is, conflict based in early development but exacerbated by—and manifested in—post-childhood
events. Our approach, while more general than symptom-oriented
therapies, is relatively specific when compared to attempts at complete reconstruction—it is repair.

In this chapter we shall discuss a number of tools of psychotherapeutic technique. Along with this, some information regarding the theory of intensive treatment, sufficient to support the
technical concepts and serve as a starting point for further
learning from teachers, supervisors and patients themselves, will
be given. Section I will address therapeutic alliance and transference, Section II the concepts of resistance and change, and
Section III techniques of understanding, making observations,
and interpretation.

I. THERAPEUTIC ALLIANCE AND TRANSFERENCE

The relationship between therapist and patient is of paramount
importance to the success of the therapeutic process. Various
parts of that relationship represent support and acceptance of the
patient, the combined front of clinician and patient against the
patient's psychopathology, replays of the sources and substance
of his conflicts and, to a greater or lesser extent, the matrix upon
which important therapeutic progress is made. The sum of this
relationship will be referred to as the *therapeutic alliance* (therapeutic relationship, working alliance), a major part of which is
the *transference*.

Transference was defined in Chapter 1, and some limitations
of the concept *vis-à-vis* process psychotherapy were briefly presented. Common forms and uses of the transference will be explored after the following discussion of the therapeutic alliance
in general.

One of the things that makes psychotherapy tolerable for
many individuals is the fact that they do not have to endure
it alone. The presence of the therapist is both a real and a fantasy
support. Although the author does not agree with the view that

much psychotherapy is "the buying of a friend," there can be no doubt that having someone to talk with and to becomes very important as anxiety-producing material is uncovered and working through becomes more difficult. The presence of various representations of the therapist within the patient's mind—all of which have to do with transference (see below)—assists the patient through difficult periods both during and between sessions. The patient feels that he is not alone and that what he is doing is acceptable.

The therapist represents and reinforces that part of the patient which is attempting to combat his psychopathology. The components of this team effort shift from time to time. Sometimes the patient's observing ego works well, and the therapist does little but watch and guide the process. At other times, the therapist is able to see things that the patient cannot. In this latter case he may communicate his observations to the patient, sometimes discussing what he feels to be the meaning of the feelings or behaviors at hand (interpretation). This collaboration is not unlike that of two business colleagues, each of whom has something important to contribute to the common goal. To carry that analogy further, one might imagine a person with access to rich and varied raw materials collaborating with another whose technical abilities and experience in the field are imperative for the creation of a finished product.

Transference

We shall discuss transference as separate from the patient's perception of the "real" qualities of the therapist and the therapeutic situation. As was stated in Chapter I, there is a continuous balance between the role of the therapist as a real person and professional, and those roles created by the patient in response to feelings directed toward the internal representations of important figures from his past. This balance is never stable, with the relative influence of each percept being related to the work being done, the patient's need to regress, his ability to regress without undue anxiety, and his need to retain the structure of the real environment.*

The real and transference parts of the therapeutic alliance coexist and affect each other, although they are artifically separated here for purposes of clarity. One way that the therapist estimates the relative content of each in a particular bit of material is by examining the appropriateness of the patient's feelings. For example:

> *Patient*: "I still feel badly about breaking that ashtray in your waiting room. Even though it wasn't very expensive, it's been on my mind ever since. I don't know what happened; I just caught it with the sleeve of my overcoat. I hope people didn't put their ashes in one of your plants after that."
>
> *Therapist*: "As you point out, the accident wasn't your fault, and you certainly have no control over whether people flick ashes onto my plants. It happened three sessions ago; why do you suppose it still brings up strong feelings?"
>
> *Patient*: "I guess I expected you to be mad. As soon as I heard it hit the floor I pictured myself in trouble. In fact, I visualized myself next to the open refrigerator door that time I dropped a dozen eggs after shopping with my mother. Funny, she didn't get mad. She just cleaned it up. She hardly ever got mad."

Comment: In the above situation there may well have been some unconscious motivation related to the breaking of the ashtray. The therapist, however, chose not to explore that point (which for this patient would have been an obscure one) and focused instead upon the patient's feelings. This line of inquiry was rewarded by the patient's association to an experience with his mother many years before, and a theme consistent with concerns about anger, guilt, and acceptance unfolded. The ashtray

---

* In reality, these circumstances do not change the transference itself so much as they change the way in which it is manifested, and those parts of it which are available for useful interpretation to the patient.

incident, including all accompanying feelings and memories, became a representation of events and relationships which were
otherwise outside the treatment setting, a firsthand example now
available to both patient and therapist for here-and-now
exploration.

*   *   *

> *Patient*: "I wish you wouldn't interrupt so much when I'm
> talking. Sometimes I'm rolling along, and when you
> speak I lose the train of thought. Sort of like when you
> answer the telephone during sessions."
>
> *Therapist*: "That can be irritating; please go ahead."

Comment: In this instance the therapist felt that the patient
had a reasonable point and was in part responding appropriately
to the real environment (e.g., the fact that the telephone rang
occasionally during sessions). He chose to comment in a way that
would encourage further production of the material at hand,
rather than exploring the patient's feelings about the interruptions, which could be done at another time.

*   *   *

"Positive transference" and "negative transference" are terms
commonly used to refer to the patient's feelings toward the therapist. Although such feelings are indeed primarily manifestations
of the transference, the complexity of the relationship often
makes the meaning of "positive" or "negative" somewhat vague.
It is more accurate to speak in terms of visible feelings, for example, describing the relationship as currently friendly, strained,
etc.

Another term in common usage is "transference cure." This
concept is frequently used to describe early improvement in the
patient, with the implication that the improvement is somehow
false or temporary. In fact, improvement may come early in the
treatment for a variety of reasons, and it may or may not remain
for a long period. That the patient has come to therapy at all implies some alleviation of conflict. He may feel relief and hope.

As the relationship with the therapist grows, he may become more hopeful that this kind of treatment will be beneficial, and he may experience real feelings of acceptance which have been absent for some time. Any of these may lead to improvement of overt symptoms, as may the wish to be compliant and rewarding to the therapist. The therapist should not begrudge the patient his new comfort nor try to remove it, although the experience should be explored in the context just mentioned.

In certain instances, the patient may wish to terminate treatment because of this symptomatic relief. The therapist should then explore with the patient what might be responsible for the improvement, sharing his view that their goal is the uncovering of underlying conflicts and thus potential improvement in other spheres as well. Even though it may seem important to keep the patient in treatment, the therapist should beware of being overly seductive or controlling. Symptoms have, after all, lessened, and if the patient is adamant about termination at this early stage, this may be an indication that future resistances will be difficult to deal with. Any termination should be supportive and not sudden or perjoratve (see Chapter 6).

"Transference neurosis" is a state in which the patient, usually as a result of lengthy and intensive experience with the therapist, centers a tremendous amount of power and responsibility around the therapist. Past conflicts are vividly recreated within the therapeutic relationship using the patient's internal representations of the therapist as substitutes for the original childhood participants. The patient's primary neurosis is replicated in, and often preempted by, that of the transference. This condition is a useful part of very intensive therapy such as psychoanalysis; however, it generally does not occur in ordinary treatment as described in this book.

Within the transference, the patient's intrapsychic representation of the therapist becomes a significant part of his feelings and therapeutic work. This occurs partly as a result of the natural course of the treatment relationship and partly as a result of the therapist's effort to decrease the real aspects of the relationship in favor of the transference (e.g., by not sharing intimate information about himself). The therapist becomes an "as if" object to a degree, although too great a deprivation of the real relationship, such as the "blank screen" therapeutic stance, is to be avoided.

The therapist's benign acceptance should not be taken to mean that absolute neutrality is desirable or possible. Silence, inactivity, or passivity will almost certainly be experienced by the patient as something other than a neutral stance. The patient, because of the transference, will perceive one feeling or another even when the therapist is being truly ambiguous. Conversely, many of the therapist's real characteristics will be made known to the patient during the lengthy course of treatment.

The transference is thus often a *displacement* whose inappropriateness to the actual situation may be seen in its quality (e.g., anger at an innocuous remark) or its intensity (e.g., feelings of intimacy in response to a simple friendly gesture). It may also be displaced onto other persons in the patient's life (e.g., a spouse or boss) and acted upon to varying degrees.

Some transference reactions are typical of virtually all patients ("general"). Others are characteristic of a given patient's development and, once understood by the therapist, contribute information specific to the conflicts and resistances that he brings to therapy.

One of the earliest signs that transference is forming is often identification with the therapist. Whether or not the patient is aware of it, the therapist is seen as some sort of ideal person. At various times this may mean he is perceived as intelligent, well-adjusted, happy, sympathetic, nurturing or aggressive. These qualities, like most others related to the transference, are essentially independent of the therapist's age, sex, or other real characteristics. The patient finds that he is able to experience some of the feelings associated with these perceived characteristics by consciously or unconsciously copying some of the traits of the therapist. This imitation (identification) affords some decrease in anxiety because of its implied safety and power. It may be manifested in something as simple as a gesture or conscious thought, or in complex behaviors such as counseling others or writing a term paper on a psychological topic.

The transference may take either of two basic forms, or combinations of both. In one the patient perceives the therapist as a *source of nourishment and love*. In the other he or she is seen as a *figure of considerable authority*. Both have obvious relationships to characteristics of important persons from the past (e.g., parents). The patient repeats, with real affect, the feelings and interpersonal experiences that he had/has with those people —or more accurately, with his internal representations of them— within the therapeutic relationship. Feelings and memories from the past and those from the real present are overlaid upon the transference. This gives therapist and patient the unique opportunity of observing firsthand a reliving of important conflicts *which do not depend upon memory or accurate reporting for their validity.*

When the therapist is being perceived as a potentially nourishing or accepting figure, the patient may respond in many ways. He may be compliant and a "good patient"; he may flatter the therapist; he may give gifts in a variety of real and symbolic ways; or he may express affection in return for that which he wishes from the therapist. Although some of these may seem ideal for the encouragement of work within the therapy, the sources of the feelings are not genuine (although the feelings are) and they may get in the way of the therapeutic work. The patient in this situation is vulnerable to feelings of jealousy (e.g., of other patients or the therapist's family), and he may be overly sensitive to even fantasied signs of rejection (e.g., the ending of the session, the therapist's silence, or cancellation of an appointment).

It is easy for the beginning therapist to confuse subtle manifestations of this kind of transference with real compliments or affection. It should be remembered that the therapist's legitimate sources of love and praise lie outside the therapeutic setting, and not in patients themselves. Even though we are all human and need the regard of others, the patient is vulnerable and the therapist's purpose is to help explore these feelings and clarify the conflicts that underlie them. By the same token, the therapist should gently be sure that the patient is aware that his friendliness does not connote friendship. If the clinician is a primary source of real gratification, some of his effectiveness as a therapist will be lost.

Perceptions of the therapist as an authority figure involve feelings that the therapist has powers with which he can gratify or frustrate, protect or take advantage of vulnerability in the patient. The therapist is seen as a person who knows about the patient and in whose hands the success or failure of the therapy resides. A mixed blessing is felt—of hope for the therapist's favor and fear of his aggressive potential.

Evidence that this kind of transference is operating may be seen in feelings of fear (which may be displaced from the therapist himself), in submissive behavior, or in the patient's caution lest he do something to offend the therapist. Some of the difficulties that these present for the therapy are obvious. If the main participant, the source of "raw materials," does only those things which he feels are safe, then little can be accomplished. As with the nourishing transference above, partial exploration of authoritarian transference feelings is necessary in order to remove some of their resistance value. In addition, the therapist can manipulate the quality and intensity of the treatment to some extent in order to prevent the development of a transference that is too intense.

The perceived benefits and potential losses to the patient from both kinds of transference overlap. For example, a person (actually an introject of that person or "object") who is seen as nourishing must also be seen as a controller of nourishment. One who gives love can also frustrate by depriving the patient of it. Feelings of anger or jealousy stemming from imagined loss of affection become dangerous, since they may, in fantasy, drive the object (person) and its gratifying powers away or even destroy it. Similarly, feelings of competition related to a perception of the therapist as successful and aggressive may highlight the patient's wishes to identify with and master that which the therapist represents, but may also obscure fantasies of weakness and fears of unacceptability should one fail to "measure up." Thus, a hierarchy of important feelings may be related to—and/or suppressed by—transference phenomena.

The therapist observes the development and machinations of the transference in the same way that he should observe all of the characteristics of the therapy: by being aware of the process involved. By attending to process even more than to the verbal content of each session and by occasionally reviewing notes from several sessions, the therapist can begin to understand *how* the patient's psychological mechanisms operate and some of their sources. *What* is in the memory and the specific words used then become secondary in importance.

Countertransference

Countertransference is similar to transference in that it represents feelings or reactions by the therapist which are related to the patient, but which cannot be completely explained by the real events which have taken place in therapy. Specifically, these are displacements onto the patient of emotional material which in actuality stems from the therapist's internal representations of important persons from his own past. In a more general sense, the term countertransference is often used to refer to any thoughts, feelings, or impulses that do not seem justified by real events in the treatment. These need not occur within the sessions, and sometimes are not aimed at the patient; however, we shall address ourselves only to those which are directly relevant to the therapy.

Many feelings that arise in the therapist are the result of the real impact or meaning of something that the patient does. These are not properly described as countertransference, even in the broad sense just mentioned. A patient may say something which is truly irritating, funny, or sad, or the patient himself may evoke apropriate feelings of pity, anger, repulsion, or the like which upon exploration have more foundation in reality than in countertransference. The way the therapist deals with these reactions is still important, of course; his susceptibility to such feelings and his ability to prevent them from impeding therapeutic progress must be considered whether they are called countertransference or not.

The most significant group of feelings that can accurately be called countertransference are those which are determined by the therapist's inner conflicts. Aggressive, sexual, and narcissistic impulses within the therapist may lead to his reacting to the patient on a basis of personal need rather than process or content of the treatment. That is, material from the patient may provoke the therapist to some action based within himself, rather than to an exploration of the sources and meanings of that material within the patient. One common presentation of this kind of countertransference reaction is the patient-therapist "battle," which may be seen in an argument during a session, in frequent mild disagreement on points of observation or interpretation, in continuous hammering by the therapist at what he erroneously feels is a resilient resistance, or even in the extension of silences during which the therapist feels, consciously or unconsciously, that he does not wish to be the one to "give in." Some of these interactions occasionally have a place in psychotherapy, but when they represent countertransference they are counterproductive in the long run.

The therapist commonly sees parts of himself in the patient. Usually, a part perceived as "bad" or otherwise symptomatic is externalized and displaced or projected onto the patient. Undue emphasis may be placed upon some particular subject which is conflictual for the therapist (sex, aggression, control, etc.). Although often rationalized as "in the patient's interest," such countertransference reactions represent unconscious gratification of the therapist or repeated attempts at mastery of his own areas of difficulty, rather than a true orientation toward psychotherapeutic progress.

Sometimes the patient's wishes to control the therapy play an important part in the reactions of the therapist. In such instances, the patient (usually unconsciously) makes the therapist feel something which the patient hopes will somehow gratify him (the patient) and reduce his anxiety. These situations do not strictly represent countertransference reactions, but are more appropriately viewed as reactions produced by the patient. Thus, when the therapist senses himself becoming bored, angry, titillated, etc., he should not only search for countertransference, but might also ask himself—and often the patient—about the possibility that the patient may have some reason for making him feel this way. Indeed, during the course of lengthy, intensive treatment, the patient becomes aware of a number of subtleties within the therapist's own makeup which can, when necessary, be used as resources for (largely unconscious) resistive manipulation.

Consistent with the above description of different kinds of countertransference phenomena, statements can be made about the probable effects of each upon the course of therapy. When the countertransference has considerable fuel from unresolved core or early derivative conflicts in the therapist, the reaction—and obstacle to treatment—tends to pervade many aspects of the treatment and is quite durable, perhaps lasting until termination. This has been described as a reaction to "generalized" countertransference.

When the therapist's reaction is a response to some particular behavior or communication which may touch upon some personal problem, but which is not overwhelmingly fueled by deep conflict (e.g., a patient's description of his reactions to a violent movie which touches feelings of anxiety in a therapist with unresolved aggressive conflicts *or* comments from a patient with marital problems similar to the therapist's own), the therapist's reaction and the effect upon the therapeutic process tend to be relatively brief. This is not to say, however, that such "specific" countertransference is benign.

Control of countertransference reactions may be discussed from three points of view: recognition of countertransference, making allowances for it, and elimination of its source. The therapist, in monitoring his own feelings and behavior, will often recognize some of the signs mentioned above. The process of the therapeutic sessions may hint that countertransference is assuming significant proportion, for example if the therapist notices a change in the quality of his participation. The material or behavior of the patient (e.g., sudden compliance, irritation, or anixety) may also reflect a reaction to some therapist behavior which has gone unnoticed.

A *caveat* should be added here: Although countertransference should be watched for, the therapist must remember that the most likely source of resistance is the patient himself. Obsessive scrutiny of one's own behavior can obscure the processes at work in the patient.

Since not all countertransference is recognizable, certain principles of therapy should be observed which allow for its existence but diminish its adverse influence. The principle of uncensored exploration of all therapeutic material, as well as the enlargement of one's fund of real knowledge about the patient, decreases the relative importance of countertransference and increases the probability that treatment decisions will be based upon well-founded deductions. In addition, the nature of long-term psychotherapy is such that specific countertransference reactions (see above) are usually diluted by the overall process.

The elimination of sources of countertransference is briefly addressed in the opening section of Chapter 2 (*The Therapist*). It must be stated that, at least in the case of general countertransference, personal psychotherapy and regular supervision are important aids. Simple introspection or review of sessions alone, while sometimes helpful, is insufficient for the beginning psychotherapist.

Many therapists describe uses to which countertransference can be put in elucidating conflict within the patient. Sometimes the therapist's personal reactions to material or behavior from the patient supply clues to the patient's motivation which would otherwise be hidden. In such instances, the therapist should try to verify the source of his or her feelings with the patient, being cautious to allow for both negative and compliant responses:

> *Therapist*: "You describe your rock climbing trips as exciting and full of important relationships with your friends. The things you've mentioned bring to my mind considerable potential danger as well. I wonder whether

that's just my own association, or whether you, too, have some feelings about the danger."

Patient: "It's not dangerous as long as you know what you're doing. I mean, you've got to have the skill and you can't take your mind off the face for an instant. It *is* scary before the climb starts, though. Sort of like the feelings my dad said he had in the Navy just before a battle. He said he never thought about the danger. Now there was a brave man."

*   *   *

In the next section, on *Resistance, Change, and Working Through* we will further explore some of the problems that transference can present. Following that, in the section on *Psychotherapeutic Technique,* some ways of using and partially interpreting the transference will be discussed.

II. RESISTANCE, CHANGE, AND WORKING THROUGH

Resistance in psychotherapy is resistance to anxiety. Resistances in any other context would be seen as defenses. Both operate to maintain a *status quo* which is extremely important to the patient and which prevents the bringing to consciousness of material which the ego feels would cause significant anxiety. Such defenses—defined as resistances when they work against therapeutic efforts—stand in the way of insight and change.

Another characteristic of resistances is that they contain considerable disguised information which is related both to the conflict that they protect and to the methods that the psyche uses in its defensive tasks. Thus resistances (1) are necessarily a part of the individual's more or less successful functioning in his environment, (2) act to stabilize the individual's entire coping system against anything which seems to threaten its integrity, and (3) are a rich source of psychotherapeutically useful information which can be used by therapist and patient in the latter's interest.

It is sometimes useful to describe different resistances/defenses in terms of the ways in which they operate within the psyche. Some common defenses categorized in this way are listed below. The combinations and relative intensities of those found in the defensive system of a given individual vary tremendously, and the content involved is unique to each of us.

> *Repression*—The preventing of conscious awareness of a thought or feeling. Repression may apply to material which has never reached consciousness or to that which was conscious at some earlier time. It is necessarily involved to some extent in all of the other defense mechanisms described below.

> *Displacement*—The substituting of one object (e.g., a person) as a target for feelings which are actually (but unconsciously) directed toward another. The object to which the feelings are displaced is emotionally safer, less likely to produce anxiety, and allows conscious expression of some of the repressed tension (impulse, wish).

> *Reaction Formation*—The replacing of an anxiety-producing thought or feeling by one which is more or less opposite to it. The conscious activity of the individual, being visibly opposite from the repressed wish, aids in keeping the latter unconscious and quiescent.

> *Projection*—The attributing of unconscious, unacceptable thoughts or feelings to some part of the external world. A painful part of the self is seen in someone else, where some of the attached affect can be experienced without threat to one's own ego.

> *Isolation of Affect*—The splitting of a thought or action from its appropriate accompanying affect. One may take place without the other (e.g., speaking of a recently deceased relative without any sign of grief), thereby protecting the ego from the threat of realizing some cause-and-effect relationship and/or becoming overwhelmed with anxiety.

> *Undoing*—A two-part activity which involves the actual or

symbolic performance of an act and then the (usually symbolic) reversal or rescinding of it. Strictly defined, the act contains disguised sexual or aggressive components, which are expressed but kept from threatening the ego by undoing.

Regression—In general, a response to ego stress in which one reverts to emotional functioning which is more primitive than that ordinarily used in coping and adaptation.

Identification—The acquiring of some of the gratifying characteristics of another person.

Introjection—The taking into oneself of characteristics of another person to such an extent that the representation of the other object becomes a part of one's self-representation.

Denial—The avoidance of awareness of some painful aspect of reality, usually by means of the creation of a fantasy which allows the avoiding to be consistent with one's perception of oneself.

Intellectualization—The binding of impulses or wishes by means of intellectual behavior. When seen as a resistance, it usually involves verbal activity which is logical but avoids strong affect or affect-laden material, thus reducing anxiety.

Rationalization—The justifying of a denial-related defense by means of logic and explanation, making repression easier for the ego.

Sublimation—The translation and modification of impulses /wishes into pursuits which are consciously acceptable to the ego and superego.

Resistances can also be categorized in terms of purpose or level of psychic involvement, utilizing concepts such as resistance to change, "character resistance," "content resistance," and transference resistance. We shall consider the first three of these together, without making differentiations among them. Transference resistance, a special characteristic of the transference relationship, will be discussed later in this section.

Resistances may present in the patient's verbal productions (quantity, quality, content, censorship, forgetting), in his behavior (lateness, cancellations, activities outside the sessions, gifts, payment of fees), in the transference, and in the overall process of treatment (e.g., isolating the therapy from real life, "flight into health"). Examples may be found in the clinical material throughout this book.

What does the therapist do once resistance is suspected or detected? When resistance is obvious, the therapist should not ignore it. He may allow it to accumulate until an observation about it is tenable within the treatment. Besides calling attention to the resistance, circumventing it may be useful. This may involve temporarily supporting the resistance in order to decrease anxiety for the time being, or working on a different therapeutic issue. As will be pointed out in the next section on *Psychotherapeutic Technique,* premature interpretation is usually of little use.

Exploration of resistances should be aimed at modifying them and thus at shifting the balance of the wish-defense conflict in the direction of allowing the wish to become closer to consciousness. Observations and interpretations should be made at a point of least resistance, addressing relatively inconsequential areas first and avoiding the underlying wish and its attendant anxiety. Deeply ingrained defenses are extremely resistant to interpretation; it may be useless to address them until late in the therapy. Often the patient himself will make these final interpretations when he is ready. Interpretations which address the wish itself may be very difficult for the patient to accept and are generally not fruitful early in treatment (see next section). In many instances, certain wishes/impulses of which the therapist may be aware are not interpreted to the patient at all.

Thus, while the therapist may use his interpretations of the patient's resistances to complete his own picture of the defensive system and the conflicts which underlie it, this information is often better used in the formulation of therapeutic procedures than as untempered material for the patient. This is not to say that work on resistances does not foster insight and improvement in the patient. Indeed, it is the most time-consuming of all the therapeutic work, and involves much that is of importance to the treatment process.

The process of a given resistance is more important than its content. The therapist is most interested in why it appeared at some particular time, how it is used, the context in which it appears, and the conflict which it symbolizes. Speculation about these issues is the first step in the modification of resistances, modification which should begin with those which are least entrenched, most recently formed ("intercurrent"), and/or acutely blocking the uncovering process. Such obstacles are frequently related to the transference (see below). Even a patient's rapid interpretation of his own resistances and defenses can be resistive, since he may thus retain control of the sessions and save himself the anxiety of an unexpected observation from the therapist.

The modification process does not always depend upon comments and interpretations from the therapist. The special nature of the therapeutic setting, with its accepting and permissive atmosphere, provides a safe place in which the patient can experiment with lessened—or different—defenses. Not only do the sessions become a testing ground for behavior which may be used outside of therapy; they also become a place in which defenses can be seen as unnecessary, at least in terms of the patient's freedom from environmental dangers and his fantasy that the therapist will protect him from overwhelming anxiety. In addition, the characteristics of the therapeutic alliance allow work on resistances to be seen as a cooperative venture of patient and therapist, further decreasing the number of sources from which anxiety may erupt should the defense begin to waver. Although the patient's struggle against facing his unconscious remains his own (i.e., the therapist does not take over his job), he has a clear and consistent ally in his work.

Resistance, like symptoms, is often perceived by the patient as "bad." The therapist should not contribute to this lowering of the patient's self-image by calling him "resistant" or by communicating pejorative feelings with respect to the patient or his progress. Exploration and explanation, not labeling, are the goals.

Transference Resistance. The transference, as well as being an important means of uncovering unconscious material, is in some ways an obstacle to the therapeutic process. When some of the patient's feelings (wishes) regarding the therapist are frustrated, negative feelings ensue and one important source of motivation and fantasy is obscured. Paradoxically, strong positive feelings which supply some internal gratification for the patient can also be resistive; denial of non-gratifying material and concomitant unwillingness to leave a comfortable stage of therapy impede the process of exploration.

Another source of transference resistance has to do with anxiety which may be brought out by strong feelings of love or hate. In this case it is not the feelings themselves which are obstacles but a resistance to experiencing affect (i.e., to experiencing the transference itself) which keeps the patient away from the developing treatment process.

Since transference resistance is an acute development (although it is a derivative of earlier experiences with relationships) and one which has taken place within the recent experience of both patient and therapist, it is relatively easy to interpret and modify. In turn, successful experiences of interpretation of transference material, with subsequent working through, aid the patient in other therapeutic work.

Working Through. Working through is the process by which the patient overcomes resistances to interpretations of repressed material. It is psychic work which allows acceptance of the repressed element (resistance or wish), and partially or completely alleviates the patient's need to repeat the resistive (defensive) mechanism which previously protected him or her from insight. The term is frequently overused. It is by definition *the work which occurs between an interpretation and the acceptance with conviction of that interpretation.*

Working through is always present in treatment, since the patient is always laboring toward insight and a more stable psychic equilibrium. It is most obviously active during the period between a specific interpretation and the loss of the resistance interpreted. The patient may at times seem to be inactive in treatment but in fact be working very hard beneath the surface, both in and outside sessions, during both waking and dreaming hours. Working through is enhanced and made more efficient by the therapist's continuing to interpret, repeating, rephrasing, and expressing differently the nature of the interpretation and resistance at hand.

The working through process permits the patient to make the transition from rejection of the interpretation or intellectual acceptance of it to real acceptance based upon his own emotional (usually affectual) experience. Following successful working through, the patient can often apply the interpretation to a new material and resistances that come under consideration.

III. PSYCHOTHERAPEUTIC TECHNIQUE: THEORY AND INTERVENTION

Before discussing at length the therapist's verbal comments, some study of his acquisition of understanding is in order. Some of this understanding comes simply from his status as an outside, objective observer. This is enhanced by the marked intensity and duration of his observations. In addition, the therapist has specific educational acumen with which to interpret to himself what he hears, and to arrive at ways to increase his understanding. Finally, the therapist's own unconscious processes—Freud's "evenly-hovering attention"—are of considerable importance. This intuitive process, which should be screened to avoid serious countertransference reactions, is assisted by learned skills with which he can organize the mass of content and detail into more general headings.

Translating the patient's comments into usable therapeutic material is sometimes simple and sometimes very difficult. Specific content may convey considerable information; indeed, words are the primary tools of therapy. Affects, the feelings with which those words are expressed, are an even better direct communication of important emotional material.

More often, verbal content is in a form of code, a resistance which allows participation in therapy but protects the patient from anxiety-filled unconscious material. As is the case with all resistances, the words and methods of communication used contain symbols of that which they protect against. Since the unconscious is truly unconscious, these symbols may be at once hidden from the patient and obvious to the therapist.

A group of statements (the *process* of a session or sessions) is required in order for the therapist to determine a consistent theme. The idea that the therapist can extract important meaning from a single statement (or dream, see below) is an exaggeration from lay misunderstanding; however, if context and process are taken into consideration, even seemingly innocuous statements may be meaningful. For example, a patient may talk about particular problems on an unspecified day in the past. Later in the session he inquires as to whether he is a burden upon the therapist. Finally, he mentions a dream in which he is sorting cancelled checks according to date. The therapist recalls that he had cancelled an appointment with the patient some weeks before and, upon inquiring, discovers that this was indeed the day on which the "problems" occurred. Subsequent material, now that the inordinate effect of the single cancelled session has been elucidated, may be rich in feelings related to acceptance, loss, and worth.

Continuity of the therapeutic process exists from session to session. The therapist should watch for and ask about the relationship of one session's material to what has occurred in previous meetings. Similarly, the patient's patterns of work and behavior over a long series of hours reflect the psychodynamic themes (wishes and defenses/resistances) that are important to him or her during that period.

In addition to wording, affect and process, certain statements can alert the therapist to the fact that the accompanying material may be particularly important. Such statements frequently are those which seem consciously to dilute the impact of the material (e.g., "Incidentally. . ." or "It doesn't really matter but. . ."). Apparently unimportant statements made just as the patient enters or leaves the session may also carry considerable meaning, since at these times the patient's resistance may be diminished and repressed material allowed symbolic expression.

The clinical vignette described above is an example of the importance that may become attached to apparently small occurrences in the therapy (cancelled appointments, the therapist's vacation, answering the telephone during a session). While these are in reality unimportant in and of themselves, they often act as "organizing pieces" (Hollender, 1965): events through which symbolically related, but much stronger, feelings may be released. Such inappropriate reactions are usually related to the transference and should be explored. If the patient denies the importance of his reaction to the event (or, conversely, if he feels he is more upset than he should be), the symbolic nature of the occurrence should be pointed out and the subsequent feelings discussed.

Freud was the first to point out the powerful therapeutic potential of the transference. He later became aware that certain kinds of work based on the transference did not have lasting effects. Agreements or apparent insights accomplished as a result of transference-related compliance are usually temporary and/or incomplete with regard to the patient's real needs. Manipulation of the patient's dependence is insufficient for useful change. For our purposes, the best uses of the transference have to do with its status as a form of therapeutic alliance, with the fact that it is a source of information for the therapist, and with the fact that interpretation of transference resistances can lead to useful insight.

Dreams. The interpretation of dreams is often looked upon by the public as the *sine qua non* of classical psychotherapy. It is clear that dreams are a rich source of symbolically disguised, otherwise unconscious, emotional material. Tension (wishes) which strives for release is kept under control during waking hours, but while the individual is asleep memories of the day's happenings ("day residue") act as a vent or conduit for release of some of this psychic pressure. Only a small proportion of dream material is remembered (the "manifest content"). Careful analysis supports Freud's impression that dreams are an important "road to the unconscious."

Another purpose of dreaming has to do with the solving of problems brought about by present or past conflict. The activity within the dream is a symbolic effort to reconcile conflicting needs and to decrease anxiety through mastery of the stylized situation that emerges.

Dreams and their interpretation should not be considered a primary focus of ordinary psychotherapy, nor should those dreams which are examined usually be considered outside of the context in which they appear. Rather, dreams are one of many sources of material for the therapeutic process. The patient may be encouraged to pay attention to his dreams; however, the author feels that the discussion of any one dream should not monopolize too much of the therapy time. The therapist's technique may involve asking the patient to explore part or all of the dream, or the therapist may remain more passive in the interest of examining the overall process of the session, including the report of the dream.

Interpretation of dreams in psychotherapy should generally focus on their meaning to the present and past of the patient, including the therapeutic experience, and not on complex or universal symbols. Similarly, although the dream may reflect deep or core conflicts, interpretations of these may be avoided unless the treatment is psychoanalytically oriented and fairly intensive, or unless the patient broaches the issue himself.

The affect and context associated with a dream are usually of more therapeutic importance than its manifest content. Since the most important context may be the transference and other things that are going on in therapy, it is frequently useful to try to relate the dream to treatment. In this regard, dreams may be seen as a special form of communication with the therapist, and one in which the patient need not take conscious responsibility for his wishes.

Patients often treat dreams as if they were alien, belonging to someone else. In order to avoid too much intellectual exercise and to encourage exploration of feelings, the therapist may point out that the dream is the patient's own, that he is its author:

> *Patient*: "In the dream I massacred all those people with a flame-thrower. I don't understand that; it's just not like me. I've never wanted to hurt anyone."

Therapist: "On the other hand, you were the author of the dream. The images, and the feelings, came from somewhere inside you."

Patient: "That makes me anxious."

Therapist: "You were anxious on Monday, before the dream, when you were talking about the people who work for you."

*   *   *

Patient: "The most striking part of the dream was being in the front of my sailboat, trying to get across the lake in a storm, and being afraid to turn back for fear of being hit by the other boats behind me."

Therapist: "It sounds as if you felt danger from ahead and pressure from behind."

Patient: "Yes. It reminds me of the therapy. I'm not sure what lies ahead, especially if things get too deep. But I've got to stick it out. I don't want to go back to the way things were before. There are lots of pressures in my life right now. I feel like I'm being pushed by my boss and my wife. Life is stormy, but you can't turn back. And even though you don't say much, I feel like I have to work hard here, maybe to please you."

Therapist: "And I sit behind you, like the boats that you felt were getting close."

*   *   *

Patient: "I had another couple of dreams this week. They're long, and they seem important."

Therapist: "You're welcome to describe the dreams and we can discuss them; however, almost all of our recent sessions have been filled with reports of dreams. In fact, they're so detailed that we've had little time to explore them. Talking about the dreams seems to be a way of filling the sessions and an obstacle to our looking into other parts of you. What do you think?"

Patient: "I thought that's what you wanted. All the psychol-

ogy books say that dreams are the only way to get to
the truth. Jung was even convinced that they represented parts of the universal consciousness."

Therapist: "Our goal is to explore *your* feelings, behaviors
and consciousness. Dreams are really only a small part
of that. Perhaps some other topics here make you
anxious."

Comment: For this patient dreams have become part of avoidance and intellectualization. Although the therapist sides
with the "logical" part of the patient, he uses the alliance
to attack the resistance which has become an obstacle to the
therapeutic process. Note that the observation is made on the
defense side of the wish-defense axis.

Interpositions and Interpretations

In this section we will discuss specific techniques designed to
make unconscious material conscious. All of the techniques
described are *verbal* ones.

We shall define as an *intervention* any statement by the therapist which has a psychotherapeutic end. Various other terms may
be used or seen in the literature, including interposition, clarification, observation, and interpretation. The former three of these
are subsumed under the heading of intervention, and will be
defined and discussed in the following paragraphs. Each particular kind of intervention has a particular use in the treatment,
and each may be more or less appropriate at different stages of
resistance; however, each plays a part in the overall goal of
meaningful insight. The therapist's ability to properly time and
phrase interventions has a great effect on their usefulness. His
ability to judge the effectiveness of interventions, especially interpretations, and to be aware of the process of working through,
is also important.

The following are five common types of interventions.

Encouragements—These include nodding, repeating the last
few words of a patient's sentence, rephrasing the pa-

tient's words, etc., in order to encourage the patient to
continue with his or her thought. Open-ended comments
such as "How do you feel about that?", "Can you continue with that thought?", or "What do you make of
that?" may also be considered encouragements.

Clarifications—These interventions are designed to clarify,
for the patient, the therapist or both, the meaning of
the patient's statement. This may be accomplished by
rephrasing or embellishing the patient's words, by asking him or her to clarify what has just been said, or
by directly stating that you do not understand what he
or she means.

*Requests for the Patient to Shift from Facts to Feelings and
Associations*—These interventions decrease emphasis on
factual content and bring the patient's attention to affect, underlying motivation, and/or process. Such statements as "How do you feel about that?", "Does that
bring any particular feelings to mind?", "How might
that be related to . . . .?", or "Do you think there
might be any other meanings, besides the ones you've
mentioned?" are examples.

The therapist may further encourage a shift from intellectualization to affect by substituting the word "feel"
for "think" in some of his statements. For example,
"What did you think of that?" might be changed to
"How do you feel about that?"

Observations—Observations relate to the patient what the
therapist has observed in his words or actions. The therapist may summarize or consolidate some characteristic
of content or process and reflect it back to the patient,
holding it up for him or her to view. For example, "That
seems related to what you said a few minutes ago,"
"You seem to be getting more and more angry as the
session goes on," "I sense a lot of sadness in your words
today," or "Your heroin use resumed just after I left
for my vacation."

Interpretations—Interpretations are statements which bring out the *latent* meaning of the patient's words or behavior. They deal with unconscious material, rather than with manifest content, seeking to explain rather than merely describe what is going on. Interpretations may address ordinary resistance, various aspects of the transference, or wishes which are being expressed through the patient's words and behavior. In practice, each of these overlaps with the other two; however, there is some need for the therapist to determine whether and how one or the other can be primarily approached.

Timing, technique, and effectiveness of interpretation vary with the specific goal sought. Some general examples: "Your concern over the puppies' health seems to reflect concern about what kind of mother you've been," "I wonder if you're going back on heroin is some sort of statement that you're angry with me for leaving you over the Christmas holidays," or "I think your anger has more to do with my going on vacation than with your difficulty finding a parking place this afternoon."

The strength or effectiveness of an intervention depends upon a number of factors. How sure is the therapist of the accuracy of his or her statement? Is the patient ready to accept the statement and make use of it? Is there clear evidence for the accuracy of the statement within the material which the patient has presented, so that he can be "convinced"? Might it be best to suggest a possible observation or interpretation, allowing the patient to expand the idea (or reject it) as he is able, rather than to make a declarative statement? Would an interpretation be harmful to the patient or the relationship at this time, especially if it is too firmly pressed? Has the therapist presented this idea many times, in different forms, without results?

The following are different ways of making statements about essentially the same patient-produced verbal material. Each might be more or less appropriate at various stages of the treatment and at various times during the process of resistance → interpretation → working through → insight/acceptance.

> —"You got high a few times." (repeat of patient's last few words)
>
> —"Why don't you tell me more about your drug activity over the holidays?"
>
> —"How did you feel about taking more heroin over the holidays?" "What do you make of it?"
>
> —"Do you think your taking the heroin had anything to do with my being gone on vacation?"
>
> —"I wonder how you felt I might react to your taking the heroin?"
>
> —"Perhaps you were angry with me (for what must have felt as if I were going away and leaving you)."
>
> —"You're telling me about taking heroin again. What else might you be telling me, either in the heroin use or in your talk about it today?"
>
> —"You felt I had left you and that made you angry enough to hurt yourself. You hurt *yourself*, although you were mad at me."
>
> —"You're angry with me for leaving, just as you were mad at Judy when she left."

The patient's ability to accept and use observations and interpretations, and hence the interpretations' effectiveness, are often poorly correlated with the therapist's idea of what is important *vis-à-vis* psychodynamics, conflict, resistance, and the like. It has been pointed out that the process of psychodynamic therapy is one of its most important characteristics and what separates it from other forms of treatment. However, interpretation of process, particularly interpretation on the "wish" side of the wish-defense axis, is quite difficult, especially early in the middle phase. Interpretation of affect is usually easier for the patient to accept, especially when some sign of the affect is consciously felt.

Observations regarding the content of psychotherapeutic material, including surface resistances that acutely impede progress, are easiest for the patient to accept. These are based on a decoding of what the patient says or the substance of a message, rather than on the communication inherent in the process (timing, affect, etc.). Such observations, followed soon by interpretations aimed at surface resistances, lay the foundation for future work on affect and process in that they (1) remove surface material, thus allowing access to that which underlies it ("peeling off one layer of the onion," to use a common analogy), (2) give the patient experience with the techniques which will be repeated over and over again during the course of treatment, and (3) allow the patient to experience success at this process, coupled with a decrease in anxiety (a sort of reward).

Timing of Interpretations. Interpretations are most useful when the patient is about to gain insight on his own. This does not mean that the therapist's intervention is superfluous; what is obvious to him may be quite unconscious, or at least suppressed, for the patient. Rather, it is at this point that the patient is most likely to accept the interpretation without major, energy-consuming resistance. Documentation to support the interpretation is frequently required to make the interpretive sequence effective. Such documentation may come from the therapist's statements and/or the patient's memory. Several different examples may be used:

> *Therapist*s "Your dream does have the aggressive characteristics you describe, but there also seems to be a strong element of control, or discomfort with unleashed aggression, implied. The boxer in the dream is very strong and very angry, but he's wearing heavy lead shoes. This seems to fit a general theme of anger, but reluctance to release it, and even more, anxiety about whether or not your various controls will be able to keep it in check. I'm thinking of your outburst of emotion earlier in the session, which was followed by the feeling that your arms were very heavy, and the brief fantasy that you were paralyzed or weak."

Poor timing of interpretations is more often merely ineffective than destructive to the treatment. Although one could discuss the possibility of a patient's being driven away by anxiety arising from a premature interpretation, more often such comments by the therapist are just denied and sloughed off.

Often observations and interpretations may be repeated over and over again, in varying forms and at varying times, with the aim of "saturating" the patient. The strong therapeutic alliance allows the patient to continue to work and to consider each intervention, until finally, with the aid of the working through process, insight becomes almost unavoidable. One might imagine a sponge upon which water drips from above. The water seems to disappear into the sponge for a long time, but finally begins to drip through on the other side. The therapist should not be dogmatic or overly forceful, and he should be fairly certain of the concepts contained in declarative interventions.

It is often tempting to summarize sessions by making observations or interpretations at the end of the hour. The therapist may discern a theme for the session and may wish to put it into perspective; however, sometimes this practice is more related to the therapist's wish to congratulate himself on his expertise than to therapeutic effectiveness. It may be more useful to interpret early in the session, allowing plenty of time to examine resistances which appear acutely, and to observe the beginning of the working through process. There is a similar temptation to summarize just before the therapist or patient leaves on vacation, giving the patient some "homework" to work on (or, unconsciously, something by which to remember the therapist). It should be remembered that interpretation is only part of the insight-producing process, and that it may be better to interpret when there is more time available. At times it seems that interpretations come at the end of a process of preparation and ripening of defenses. More accurately, the interpretation is at the middle of a particular bit of work, preceding the working through which leads to the making conscious of previously unconscious material.

Interpretations must be in a form that the patient can tolerate and work with. Even with the best timing, multiple, confusing, or psychological sounding interpretations may not be workable for the patent. Similarly, the anxiety that the interpretation produces should allow optimal energy for working through and should not be so uncomfortable that insuperable defenses are raised. The best accepted interpretations contain only one basic concept (although there may be several examples of that concept) and are as unambiguous as possible. In practice, the latter often refers to a situation in which environmental (reality) events can be excluded from the list of ways in which the patient may resist. In addition, lack of ambiguity also refers to the need to address only one aspect of the conflictual or resistive material at a time, even though the therapist may be aware of many meanings, motivations, or causes for a particular set of feelings or behaviors (overdetermination). Thus the therapist might say:

> *Therapist*: Your behavior in each of these instances has seemed almost compliant. Your being liked and accepted seems very important on the job, at home, and here with me."

rather than

> *Therapist*s "This compliant behavior that you describe seems to indicate a need to be accepted and liked. Underneath that wish to be liked may be a fear that you'll be misunderstood and left, perhaps even that people will fear your aggressive impulses."

What if the therapist's interpretation or other statement is simply erroneous? As mentioned above, the interpretation should not be dogmatic or overly forceful. Objections from the patient should be reasonably considered; if an error is discovered, it should be acknowledged (although the therapist should not be inordinately ambivalent about his interventions). Such acknowledgment should be brief and straightforward, according the patient appropriate respect but avoiding apology or guilt. The interpretation was, in all likelihood, not made without some reasons; the characteristics and material which led to the intervention may be explored.

The therapist's own feelings, perhaps countertransference, should ordinarily not be explored during the session. There is no need for a *mea culpa* stature. At the same time, the therapist should not attempt to be a stereotypic version of the perfect clinician. In this, as in other treatment situations, his humanness and individual style need not be overly suppressed.

The patient's response to observations and interpretations may convey a great deal of information to the therapist. The therapist soon learns what kinds of response in a given patient—verbal and nonverbal—indicate acceptance of interpretations, rejection of them, accuracy, or error. Silence, a common response, often indicates an incorrect interpretation and/or disappointment at not being understood; however, it may also mean that the new information is being pondered and digested. Similarly, a particular patient may quickly change the subject (or affect) following interventions which are anxiety-producing. This may also occur when the patient perceives disinterest, error, or usurping of his feelings by the therapist.

> *Patient*: "I'm not making sense. I feel disappointed."
> *Therapist*: "Fred isn't gratifying you . . . nor am I in many ways you'd like."
> *Patient*: "No, that's not it. I need him around, and I know he's not going to stay when he finds out about my record."
> *Therapist*: "You'd like to be sure there's someone there to care for you; just as the thought of my going out of town makes you wonder whether I'll really be coming back."
> *Patient*: "I'm tired. Dragged out. . . You don't understand."

Comment: In this case, the therapist erroneously focused upon process material related to general dependency needs and threatened loss, rather than upon the immediate issue (and content) at hand. The patient's response indicated that she was not ready for this sort of intervention. From her point of view, and to that session's temporary detriment, the therapist "didn't understand."

*   *   *

When avoidance or resistance to an intervention is seen, the therapist should examine the patient's next comments for symbolically-related material. Even though avoidance and denial may be at work, the verbalizations which follow almost always contain symbolic reflections of the same defense mechanisms which have been seen in other parts of the treatment (and of the patient's life). Such material is never random or coincidental, although its relationship to the subject at hand may be so distant that it should not be further explored or interpreted. Some such material, even that which is seemingly resistive, may be part of the working through process which will eventually lead to acceptance and insight.

> *Therapist*: "You seem to see those things in black or white. It's as if all confrontations, including some here in the sessions, were dangerous ones."
>
> *Patient*: (after a long silence) "I was daydreaming . . . My stomach is bothering me."
>
> *Therapist*: "The daydreaming is a response to my comments, isn't it? An escape and perhaps a suppressing of some difficult feelings."
>
> *Patient*: "I guess that's why I was having a pleasant daydream. About seducing a woman."

Comment: The patient's response to the intervention/interpretation indicates resistance to it and defense against the loss of that which the previous material was protecting (including feelings of confrontation). Both the form and the content of the resistances (daydream, stomach discomfort) hold disguised information about the material interpreted, i.e., escape, anger, anger held back (inside), control and engulfment (seduction).

The patient's participation in the interpretation of material should generally be encouraged whenever possible. This may mean allowing the patient himself to make interpretations when he is able, or allowing him to begin the working through process by expanding upon observations and interpretations already made. Some patients, especially those who are already psychologically sophisticated, regularly make interpretations before the therapist does. Often the patient's interpretation is more or less different from that which the therapist was planning to make, but there is a temptation to allow it to stand since it has come from the patient himself. If this occurs with regularity, the resistive nature of the behavior should be noted (and perhaps interpreted itself). Such resistances include those related to controlling the sessions, competing with the therapist, and/or defending against the surfacing of alternative material which has risen to near-consciousness.

Of the large amount of material which might be observed or interpreted that one finds in a given session, only a small fraction is commented upon. As mentioned earlier, most interpretations focus upon events or behaviors which lead to difficulty, either in the treatment or in the patient's current life situation. The presence of these is often communicated as material which is unusual, self-destructive, or anxiety-producing, and may be reflected in verbalizations, thoughts, feelings, or actions. Interpretation of defense (especially resistance) is usually more effective than, and should take precedence over, interpretation of conflict (particularly wishes or impulses), especially early in the treatment. Although it may be more difficult for the patient to accept, once a strong therapeutic alliance has been established, successful interpretation of process will in the long run be more useful than interpretation of content. Resistance should be suspected if the therapist finds himself so busy observing or interpreting minutiae that larger issues of affect and treatment process are consistently postponed.

All interpretations threaten the patient with loss, in that they suggest (and press for) change from the patient's previous frames of reference and modes of defense. The patient must gather up a certain amount of courage in order to give up some of his old ways and feelings. A certain amount of discomfort (anxiety) with the prior mechanisms may be required in order to fuel or motivate such change. A number of writers (e.g., Tarachow, Weiner), considering this loss experience, address the likelihood of mild, temporary depression following interpretations which are correct and properly timed.

Interpretations may be perceived as implying to the patient that his present psychological mechanisms are ineffective or unrealistic. If the patient feels he is being criticized for having such foibles, then the intervention may be seen as an attack. Depending upon the status of negative and positive effects of the transference, the patient may feel a blow to his self-esteem. Thus, some resistance to the interpretation may be related to defense of the self, in addition to that of the specific issue at hand.

Exploration and Interpretation of Transference

It will be remembered that the primary sign of transference, especially transference resistance, in the patient's material is *inappropriateness*, particularly inappropriateness of the intensity of the patient's affect (either increased or muted).

> *Patient*: "I hear ice clinking back there. It sounds like you're drinking something"...(the patient then associates feelings of anger with hearing the therapist drink)..."You're probably doing it on purpose, at least clinking the ice, to have some effect on me."
>
> *Therapist* (establishing real issue): "Actually, someone had some extra Coke and offered it to me just before you came. But you obviously have some feelings attached to my drinking and to the sound of the ice."
>
> *Patient*: "I see you laid back, relaxed, and me all alone. I lie here and suffer and sweat."
>
> *Therapist*: "I have Coke and you don't, and I haven't offered any to you. That sounds like feelings of being treated unfairly even though, as you point out, you are working and suffering and deserve to feel good."

Patient: "Yeah. Work is going all right, though, and I'm not being treated any different from anyone else. It's hot there, too. I treat everyone with respect, even the animals. Today one of the technicians had a problem and I listened to her for almost an hour. There's that sound again. Are you still there?"

Therapist: "I think you're concerned that I might not be attending to you 100%, while in your fantasy I sip my drink and relax."

Patient: "You're entitled. I have a Coke when I'm working, and it doesn't keep me from doing my job. So why should I feel mad. Mad. I had an image of a big spot on your three-piece suit. Maybe it's Coke. It won't come out and your wife is going to be mad. I know you're not married. Your dog will be mad. Mad dog. God dam spelled backwards. God damn I'm mad. *Did* you clink the ice just to see what I'd do? No, you don't play games with your patients."

Comment: A number of transference-related feelings arose in response to the sound of ice softly clinking in a plastic cup. While some therapists might feel that the patient has a legitimate reason to feel either slighted or pre-empted, most would agree that the quality—and certainly the intensity—of the reaction is inappropriate to the real situation. What occurred was the opening of a window into feelings of isolation, deprivation, nonacceptance, and (closer to the surface) anger related to all of these. As the sesson continued, the therapist chose the theme which seemed most involved in current resistance and affect (anger) for further development and eventual interpretation.

*   *   *

Although signs of the transference and its accompanying resistances are almost always noticeable for the therapist, many therapists feel the transference should generally not be interpreted unless it produces significant resistance to therapeutic progress, or until it is of considerable intensity and interpretation, so that interpretation can offer useful information to the patient. Especially in ordinary (as opposed to psychoanalytically oriented) psychotherapy, most transference interpretation should have as its aim clarification rather than deep exploration. The goals of this kind of therapy are exploration and modification of derivative conflict, rather than of core conflict. By the same token, although regression will naturally occur and may be useful in limited quantities, profound and sustained regression is neither necessary nor desirable for these purposes.

The general procedures for interpretation of transference are the same as those for interpretation of ordinary resistance and conflict. Interventions concerning direct and easily visible expressions of transference should be made before attempting to interpret subtle or indirect material. Negative transference material is by and large more visibly resistant than is positive transference, and thus may be easier to interpret; however, since resistances are also associated with positive feelings, the latter will eventually need to be addressed if therapy is lengthy and intense. Since interpretations can be perceived as expressions of interest, or at least of attention, and since the transference is an affect-laden experience for the patient, exploration of positive transference may be felt as reward, friendliness, reassurance, frustration (of the fantasied relationship), or even seduction.

Except for preventing its overdevelopment, the therapist should avoid manipulating the transference, consciously or unconsciously. The elements of transference will come naturally, from the patient and not from the therapist. Thus, a clinician who is overly reassuring, friendly, or critical may be artificially influencing the therapeutic process and adding confusing environmental variables to the therapeutic arena. Another form of manipulation of transference, more a psychotherapy stereotype than common clinical practice, has to do with the idea that the therapist should attempt to manipulate the fine points of the patient's experience, including the transference. Patients and laymen frequently say "You know what I'm thinking," or "I'm angry, but I know that's the way you're trying to make me feel" (see clinical example above); however, these feelings should be in the patient's fantasy rather than based upon any action the therapist has really taken. One should merely keep a general, inexorable emphasis on progress, the development of insight, and the thwarting of resistances.

When anxiety rises above the optimum level necessary for motivation and threatens the patient's ability to accept interpretations, work through, or otherwise participate in therapy, then some intervention is necessary. Such situations are sometimes best overcome by circumvention rather than interpretation. The conflict being considered will always resurface at a later time, perhaps in a different context, when resistance may be lower. This concept of the reemergence over and over of dynamically identical material throughout the treatment not only makes it possible for the therapist to wait for the most effective opportunity for interpretation, but it also establishes the fact that, should an opportunity for intervention be missed (or misused), there will be many other chances in the future.

In active therapy there is an almost constant shift between past and present, between real events and fantasy, and between memories of past relationships and the current transference experience. Material which limits itself to only one of these dimensions for any length of time may indicate stagnation and resistance. For example, verbalizations of real events should be addressed by the therapist and woven into the overall process.

> *Patient*: ". . .As usual, I disagreed with him in a polite way."
> *Therapist*: "In a 'polite' way."
> *Patient*: "Yes. There was no need to get upset. It wouldn't do any good, wouldn't change his mind. I guess I'm usually polite. Sort of a civilized person."
> *Therapist*: "I wonder what the politeness means. Any fantasies about what happens when you are, or aren't, polite?"

Comment: The therapist attempted to enlarge the sphere of the current, reality-oriented material by suggesting fantasy. He might also have asked about memories of past politeness, or about ways in which politeness (or lack of it) appears in the therapy sessions.

Crises in Therapy

We have not addressed any of the many crises which the patient may go through during the course of therapy. Emotional disability which requires serious interruption of the therapy (e.g., change to strong support or crisis intervention) is uncommon in the patients who are most suited to intensive psychotherapy, at least by the students and beginning psychotherapists for whom this book is intended. Of course, the patient may feel that he is in crisis, and should be treated in the appropriate context *vis-à-vis* session content and process. Issues such as severely overwhelming anxiety (as might be seen in the "borderline" patient), disabling depression, suicide attempts, or psychotic decompensation require special considerations which are, in large measure, not addressed herein. The reader is encouraged to consult other texts and discuss such potential situations with an experienced supervisor.

CHAPTER 6

Termination

✱✱✱

The ending of a course of psychotherapy is technically and psychodynamically complex. The manner in which treatment is closed is very important to the lasting success of the work done during the initial and middle phases.

There is often a temptation—for both therapist and patient —to make termination a brief affair. After all, the major work has been done; the decision to end therapy has been made. Why waste time and the patient's money prolonging things?

Resistance to playing out the hand of the entire treatment process is just that: resistance. Careful thought leads one to the conclusion that therapy is not complete after middle phase. The termination phase is necessary to wrap up work started earlier, to integrate the entire process of treatment and to resolve the complex therapeutic relationship that has formed. The therapist must assist the patient with this transition, supporting his progress and working to avoid any regression sufficient to undermine his psychotherapeutic accomplishments. All of these involve energy and, inevitably, some loss. Both, as we have seen, lead to resistance.

The patient may find it difficult to see or express signs of therapeutic progress that, to him, hasten the end of treatment. Such resistance must be watched for, especially as new symptoms arise (or old ones resurface) during termination. Postponement of closure, when based upon this resistance or upon the feeling that enthusiasm for termination may offend the therapist (a sign of unresolved transference), should not be allowed.

The amount of time and energy which should be devoted to termination is greatly proportional to the strength of the therapeutic relationship and the fragility of the patient's improvement. These are, in turn, often proportional to the duration and intensity of the treatment (although this is not always the case). If one sees a patient for an agreed-upon contract of 15 weekly meetings, for example, formal termination may involve only two or three sessions, with some mention being made of the approaching end of therapy sometime after the halfway point is reached. More intensive work, say, several months at two or three times a week, requires much more termination time. Lengthy analytically-oriented treatment may allow two or three months for the ending process.

In some forms of treatment and with some kinds of patients not addressed here, intense and often almost symbiotic relationships can form within only a few sessions. The rule in those cases is to end the relationship gently and appropriately, using the transference and the ego strengths of the patient as measures rather than the number of sessions. With all patients, no matter what the setting or treatment format, the important thing is to *think about* termination and not to let expediency or resistance (the patient's or one's own) prevent good closure of the therapeutic experience.

Termination, like other life events and the therapy itself, is a dynamic process. Given a reality-based event such as the setting of a date for the end of therapy, the patient with a relatively strong ego immediately begins to adapt to the changes at hand.

In a sense, time itself is an important ally, with the therapist giving support and preventing a too precipitous withdrawal, while the patient works through stages sometimes not unlike those associated with classic loss and grief: denial, anger, bargaining, and acceptance. However, the therapist has a responsibility for making this period not only one of acceptance and cutting of ties, but also of continued growth and preparation for the future.

In uninterrupted therapy, the termination phase often begins when the conflicts which the therapist feels are goals for resolution have clearly responded to treatment. Such conflicts may represent pragmatic, reality-oriented goals or may be more psychodynamic in nature. In this and previous discussions we have referred to the latter. When the therapeutic work is nearing completion—but not while strong resistances are still at work—the therapist should bring this fact to the attention of the patient. Then, over the next several sessions, a schedule for termination should be mutually agreed upon. Below are some examples of hypothetical vignettes, along with some potential patient comments.

> *Therapist*: "The past few weeks of work indicate that you've made a lot of progress in understanding your feelings."
> *Patient*: "I know. I was thinking that last week."
> *Therapist*: "More importantly, your comments, your behavior, even your dreams seem to reflect some basic changes in the way you feel about yourself. I wonder if our work is just about complete."
> *Patient*: "Maybe, but I'd like to be more sure of things before I stop."
> *Therapist*: "Of course. Why don't we talk about it for a couple of sessions."
>
> *Therapist*: (2 weeks later): "It's settled then. Our last session will be eight weeks from today; that's July 20th."
> *Patient*: "Sounds good. A little scary but good."

*   *   *

Therapist: "You know you've done a lot of work during these months; in fact we've worked together for over a year. I think we should begin to think about eventually stopping the therapy."

Patient (anxiously): "You mean I've gone as far as I can go? I still have trouble with my husband you know, and my headaches came back last week."

Therapist: "I'm certainly not implying that you can't 'go further,' and I don't mean that we should quit this week. I do feel that your work thus far represents a sort of package of progress, of understanding and change in your ways of dealing with things, and it seems time to relax from our formal sessions."

Patient: "But my symptoms aren't gone. My friend's psychoanalysis lasted four years."

Therapist: "As we discussed earlier, there may be many causes for symptoms: old habits, influence from outside of yourself, even your continuing to choose them as a way of coping. The important thing is the deeper result which we've seen in your feelings and behavior. And incidentally, the end of therapy doesn't necessarily mean an end to change."

Patient: "When will we stop?"

Therapist: "Not for some time yet. Why don't we talk about it for a few sessions and then agree on a date."

In the first example, the patient shares, on many levels, the feeling that therapy is nearing completion. The therapist is aware of the complex feelings associated with termination and suggests mutual participation in the final decision. Two weeks later definite termination plans have been made, plenty of time is allowed, and a firm date is set for the last session.

In the second example, the patient is more reluctant to give up the therapy. She raises a number of resistive ideas, some seemingly realistic and others clearly related to fantasies and magical expectations about therapy and the therapist. The therapist, realizing the nature of these and recalling work done over the previous year, believes firmly that further intensive work is not indicated at this time. Some goals of treatment have been met; others may have been found inappropriate or unrealistic for this patient at this time, especially since, unlike her friend, she is not in psychoanalysis and is aware of that fact. The therapist, as he has in the past, reassures the patient concerning the difference between symptom relief and other signs of worthwhile therapeutic work. While not denigrating the symptoms' importance, he attempts to place them in perspective, just as he has as they have come and gone with other threats of loss over the year of therapy. Finally, an air of mutual participation is fostered and the setting of a firm termination date is implied.

Success in psychotherapy should be seen in terms of progress toward objectives rather than their complete attainment. Extension of treatment until all goals have been reached is often impossible and, in any event, may not be in the patient's best interest. For example, a particular patient might realize considerable, if incomplete, benefit in two years of treatment but might require much longer to accomplish further significant change. It is logical to consider termination as the "cost/benefit" ratio increases.

CRITERIA FOR TERMINATION

There are many statements in the literature which address the criteria for beginning termination. Termination should be considered when the patient is feeling and functioning better *as a result of fundamental changes in derivative conflicts and in ego protection mechanisms (defenses)*. The patient should be equipped to continue working on his own, and the therapeutic relationship should be moving toward a resolution in which its real aspects increase in proportion to transference fantasies. This does not mean an increase in friendship or intimacy with the patient; rather, the real characteristics of the relationship that have been present throughout therapy now become a clearer part of treatment, as the transference becomes less necessary and is slowly given up.

Of course, the patient may recognize the need for termination before the therapist. Some therapists rely to some extent upon the patient's own feeling that he or she has completed most of the therapeutic task. In the author's opinion, the responsible therapist takes an active part in this decision, being aware of the possibility that the patient is simply expressing resistance to further, indicated treatment.

The patient may suggest termination for a variety of reasons in addition to the resistance-related ones just implied. He may feel he has accomplished as much as is possible for the time being, or that the benefits of new insight no longer outweigh the many costs of remaining in therapy. Some patients monitor their progress closely and inquire about how much longer the therapist thinks treatment will be needed. Although all of these may represent resistance, they may also signify an appropriate time for termination to begin.

The therapist must be aware of his or her own desires either to be rid of the patient or to keep him in therapy. Countertransference feelings, as well as simple needs such as fees or trainee credit, must be watched for and sublimated in the interest of the patient.

One of the therapist's main tasks in termination is to *decrease the fantasy portion of the transference in favor of the real person-to-person relationship*. The more successful the shift in this balance, the easier it is for the patient's ego to assume greater autonomy, replacing the representation of the therapist in areas in which the latter may have been symbolically substituted for the patient's own coping mechanisms (ego or superego). Reminders of personal responsibility (which really has been present all along) through mutual patient-therapist participation are helpful in preventing, for example, a compliant atmosphere which would contribute to the tendency to regress in the hope of postponing the termination/loss.

The setting of a firm ending date is useful in a number of ways. It unambiguously states the therapist's feeling that termination is appropriate. Ambivalence in the patient should not be reflected in the therapist; for example:

Patient: "This new job is bringing back a lot of my old symptoms (conflicts/feelings), and we only have a few more sessions to go. I've been thinking that I could sure use another month or so of therapy, just to get things ironed out."

Therapist: "Your feelings about the job are important, but it also sounds like you have some anxiety about termination."

Patient: "Yeah. I thought this part would be easy. I guess I've really gotten used to coming here—seeing the office, even that picture over the bookcase."

*   *   *

Patient: "Oh, by the way, I thought I'd visit my sister and her family in Florida next month. I'd be gone for a couple of weeks and I suppose that would mean postponing our last session, but she seems so lonely, and I haven't seen my nephews since I started therapy."

Therapist: "The trip idea seems to have come up rather suddenly. Might it have anything to do with our ending the therapy?"

Patient: "It seems like everything I say has 'something to do with therapy.' I suppose this does too, but I really want to see Fran. Isn't that all right?"

Therapist: "As we've discussed, the decisions are yours to make and neither would be 'right' or 'wrong.' I think it is important, though, that we keep the same ending date regardless."

Patient (irritated): "I'll have to think about it. It'll mean cancelling my reservations, and they're hard to get this time of year."

In the first example, anxiety about termination leads to ambivalence in the patient. The therapist chooses not to focus on the job (a new issue) or on old symptoms (which have been previously explored and understood). Instead, termination feelings are suggested as the source of anxiety and the patient begins to bring out feelings associated with separation and loss. The ending date is not specifically mentioned but it is clear that the reality of termination has not changed.

In the second example, anxiety and ambivalence, stemming from feelings very similar to those of the first patient, show themselves in other, somewhat less adaptive ways. The patient is less receptive to insight and, in fact, has acted out by making travel reservations. Some psychodynamics of her basic character and of termination issues are symbolized in comments about the fantasied trip. The patient is given the opportunity to connect these with the ending of therapy and the therapist is convinced that she has the intellectual understanding to do so. When she resists this and asks for the therapist's opinion/orders/blessing, the therapist gently but firmly returns responsibility to her. She reacts with the anger of frustration, but is able to seriously consider cancelling her acting-out behavior.

If the therapist in either case above were to have postponed termination, the most important result would have been a communication to the patient of ambivalence about the patient's improvement and readiness to stop therapy. The therapist is not being mean by refusing a few more sessions, any more than he is mean if he, in the patient's interest, refuses to write an unneeded prescription. He is keeping his promise and carrying out the endgame of a long and complex process. He is acting on the basis of evaluation of months or years of clinical evidence, and is not unduly swayed by short-term resistances.

In an effort to postpone loss—of the therapeutic relationship or of parts of one's own self-image—symptoms may return, acting-out may occur, ambivalence may appear, and myriad feelings may be displaced and projected. Such patterns of coping will be reflected in both the original defense mechanisms of the individual and the ones which represent modification and emotional change by the therapy. As such they can be interpreted to the patient. Often, resistances which were resilient during the middle phase are more easily handled during termination. Negative transference, for example, can sometimes be expressed more readily as closure approaches.

These interpretations should be done in a positive manner; a patient who has reached this phase of treatment has accomplished a great deal, whether or not his—or the therapist's—initial goals have been completely attained. The patient receives credit and credit is due.

Another useful aspect of setting a specific termination date has to do with the mapping and observation of termination patterns. As we have seen, the complexity of this last phase can be confusing to the patient and therapist. A stable endpoint helps both persons to translate feelings and behaviors into a structure, which leads in turn to increased understanding and direction and to lowered anxiety. Shifts in the termination date undermine this stability to a greater or lesser degree.

An increase or decrease in symptoms is one of the things that can best be understood when placed against a backdrop of such structure. It is common to see symptoms increase soon after the issue of termination is first broached. In some individuals, notably those similar to the second patient in the above vignettes, symptoms increase in intensity as the termination date nears. After an unambivalent termination, symptoms often decrease markedly. When termination is ambivalent, however, fantasies of returning to the therapy/therapist may give rise to continuation of symptoms which, magically, are associated with attracting the object which has been lost.

It should be emphasized that the patient who stops treatment does not stop thinking or working. Changes that have taken place continue to influence the person's feelings and growth. New patterns of ego defense make it possible for him or her to view events and memories differently, sometimes more realistically. The therapeutic process has to some extent been incorporated and is available for examination and use by the former patient when defenses allow. He has a different, more effective set of tools with which to deal with both internal conflicts and external problems.

In some patients, the representation of the therapist remains as an influential image (not just a memory) in the psyche for some time. This is often unavoidable and can be useful; however, it is the therapist's goal to generally shift away from such use of the transference. He or she is not omniscient or omnipresent; continued fantasies of magical strength and dependency are rarely in the interest of the neurotic patient. The transference is to be resolved, not merely submerged.

FORCED AND PREMATURE TERMINATIONS

For many clinicians, especially new therapists and those who work with transient populations, the luxury of truly open-ended treatment and natural termination is the exception rather than the rule. Setting aside the case of a patient whose resistance causes him to leave treatment abruptly in an earlier stage of therapy, we can examine several kinds of early termination experience which can, with care, be turned to advantage for the patient. When the end of treatment is predictable well ahead of time, as in the case of a trainee's time-limited residency or practicum, it will be referred to as "forced." When it is not predicted, as with sudden military or vocational transfer to another city, it will be called "premature."

Forced termination is really an example of what some call "contract" psychotherapy. It occurs when some outside factor or event limits treatment plans from the outset. The trainee who knows he must leave the clinic after a number of months, the patient who is a student or trainee himself, or the clinic setting which encourages time-limited therapy—all require planning of the treatment to best take advantage of the period available. In such cases the temptation to continue the middle phase of therapy at the expense of the termination phase must be restricted.

In forced termination the course of treatment can at least be planned and major problems usually need not occur. This is often not the case with premature endings. What can the therapist do when faced with a patient who must quit therapy?

Since part of the therapist's job is to assist the patient with his balance of reality and resistance issues, the first step is often to determine whether or not termination really must occur. The patient who appears to be presenting a crucial reality situation may actually be presenting a resistance, or even a test of the therapist.

> *Patient*: "I just found out I'm being seriously considered for that vice-presidency of the Western Division. It'd mean moving to Utah, but I just can't see turning down that salary, the fringe benefits and clean air for the kids. It's just what I've worked for for years."
>
> *Therapist*: "Sounds like quite an opportunity."
>
> *Patient*: "Oh, it is. Vice-president at 38! In my business that's almost unheard of. Of course, I'd continue therapy. Do you know any good psychologists in Salt Lake?"
>
> *Therapist*: "I'm sure there are many. Tell me, how do you feel about being considered for vice-president?"
>
> *Patient*: "Great! It's a real pat on the back. I feel accepted; like they're finally recognizing my hard work." (Pause)
>
> *Therapist*: "And what about your hard work here, in the therapy?"

Comment: In this example the therapist quickly recognizes the patient's need for acceptance and specialness. The patient may or may not decide to move away, but the decision will be reached after reality and resistance factors have been thoroughly explored. The therapist has neither pushed the patient away nor seduced him to stay. In the following vignette the choice is clearer.

> *Patient* (at the beginning of the hour): "I'm afraid I have some important news. Frank is being transferred to a NATO division in Heidelberg. He has to report there next month and the kids and I must follow within 60 days."
>
> *Therapist*: "That's quite a piece of news."
>
> *Patient*: "I know. There wasn't any warning. He got his orders day before yesterday. We talked about it a lot. We both have ties here but he can't turn down the

assignment. Anyway, that's the kind of life we elected when he signed on. I suppose I could stay here—there's dependent housing on the Base and I could keep my social work position—but all in all it looks like another overseas move."

Therapist: "I agree. From what you've said there seems little reason for you to stay behind with the children if your husband's transfer is inevitable."

Patient: "We'll get confirmation within a few days. This is a real shock; just when I was getting used to therapy. This place is almost a second home to me. . ."

Comment: The patient has presented a situation which, short of blatant therapeutic seduction, must lead to termination within two months. Within the first few sentences she has communicated her knowledge and acceptance of the reality situation, as well as at least one major consideration for focus during the termination phase (frequent losses, military moves, lack of permanence of gratifying objects and relationships).

*   *   *

With the patient in the latter example, the therapist must first set the stage as he or she would for any other termination. That is, after confirmation of the move a termination date should be set and relatively rapid shifts made toward resolution of the therapeutic relationship. Since the goals of treatment have not all been reached and some dynamic explorations have been interrupted midstream, more than the usual attention must be paid to sealing off some emotional pathways that cannot be completely treated in the time allowed. Vulnerability can be reduced while credit and support are given for work which the patient has done during the past months or years.

As in the case of natural termination, growth can continue after the sessions have stopped, especially if the transference is properly resolved. Should the patient desire further therapy—or should the therapist recommend it—such a suggestion can be made, with or without a letter of referral, since in this case termination is not the result of a completed therapeutic experience.

Some therapists taper the frequency of sessions as termination approaches, much as the intensity of the treatment is gradually reduced. Others feel that this is rarely necessary and may add an unnatural flavor to the last sessions. Similarly, the patient who is accustomed to reclining may begin to sit up during the final meetings, although the position assumed is less important than the process and feelings involved.

As the final hour approaches, most patients have developed a realistic, optimistic view of the times which lie ahead. The future is a legitimate topic of discussion, and "discussion" rather than "therapy" is appropriate. Some patients may ask if it is all right to call you by your first name or give you a gift, perhaps one which was earlier explored as an acting-out behavior and turned away. Such activity may be confusing for the therapist.

Some gifts, cards, or a brief goodbye hug are perfectly acceptable provided they are given and received in a context of token gratitude and finality. Psychodynamic implications, always present, may be secondary in the overall atmosphere of termination. The therapist must, however, try not to reinforce attempts to hang onto the therapy and/or avoid resolution of the transference, especially in patients in whom primitive emotional characteristics are prominent. It is unfair to the patient to hold out false hopes of a symbolically lasting relationship by encouraging, overtly or subtly, gifts, letters, continued friendship, and the like. For example, although the patient who is a medical student may make the transition from "patient" to "colleague," it might be unwise for the ex-therapist to supervise him or her during a later residency. Similarly, one would probably decline a dinner invitation from a family in which he has seen a member in intensive treatment.

After termination, one occasionally hears from former patients. If such calls or letters represent vestiges of unresolved transference, they should be handled with some care. The first couple of communications should be acknowledged, for example by means of brief, professional, typed letters or returned telephone calls which sympathize with the person's concerns, allude to termination, and support his or her ability to deal with things alone. If referral to another therapist has been made, the patient must be encouraged to take matters up with him or her. Further communications of this type indicate incomplete termination and/or relatively deep disturbance. Except in the case of a schizoid or borderline patient, or one who is acutely depressed, contact should be ceased, perhaps with referral to another therapist. Re-entry into treatment with the patient is sometimes tried but is likely to result in confusion and elaboration of magical expectations rather than in the resolution wished for by the patient (or therapist).

More often, given a patient with good ego strengths who has progressed satisfactorily to termination, communications are short and appropriate. Notice of a new job or wedding or a brief holiday greeting is pleasant to receive. The former may suggest some equally brief congratulatory reply; the latter requires no acknowledgment. The ex-patient is sending a token, albeit with some meaning if we wish to search for it, but one which is a fitting contact from a person who sees his life—joys and tragedies and otherwise—as his own.

BIBLIOGRAPHY

❧❧

BRENNER, C. *An Elementary Textbook of Psychoanalysis.* New York: International Universities Press, 1973.

CHESSICK, R. D. *The Technique and Practice of Intensive Psychotherapy.* New York: Jason Aronson, 1974.

COLBY, K. M. *A Primer for Psychotherapists.* New York: Ronald Press, 1951.

DEWALD, P. A. The process of change in psychoanalytic psychotherapy. *Archives of General Psychiatry,* 35:535-542, 1978.

FREUD, S. *Standard Edition,* various volumes. London: Hogarth Press.

GREENSON, R. R. *The Technique and Practice of Psychoanalysis, Vol. I.* New York: International Universities Press, 1967.

HARTMANN, H. *Ego Psychology and the Problem of Adaptation* (translated by D. Rapaport). New York: International Universities Press, 1958 (from "Ich-Psychologie and Anpassungsproblem," 1939.).

HOLLENDER, M. H. *The Practice of Psychoanalytic Psychotherapy*. New York: Grune & Stratton, 1965.

KLEIN, M. *Contributions to Psychoanalysis: 1921-1945*. London: Hogarth Press, 1948.

MOORE, B. E. and FINE, B. D. *A Glossary of Psychoanalytic Terms and Concepts*. New York: American Psychoanalytic Association, 1968.

TARACHOW, S. *An Introduction to Psychotherapy*. New York: International Universities Press, 1963.

WEINER, I. B. *Principles of Psychotherapy*. New York: John Wiley & Sons, 1975.

WHITE, R. B. and GILLILAND, R. M. *Elements of Psychopathology: The Mechanisms of Defense*. New York: Grune & Stratton, 1975.

INDEX